DEDICATION

I would like to dedicate this book to the Salt of the Earth people discovering the **SUPER** *inside to create the* **FANTASTIC** *outside.*

The SUPERFANTASTIC Process

Becoming a Salt of the Earth Leader

2021

FOREWORD

I am a process person. If there are steps to take to get to a desired result, I am taking notes. By the same account, if there are no defined steps or processes to attain a desired result, I will either create one on paper (or rather my computer) or in my head. If there is no process, it becomes so easy for me to start wandering and creating random thoughts with very little organization.

Things are easier for me to absorb when there is a process by which to follow. It helps me visualize the path, picture the result, light up the path and stay locked on my desired result. Understandably the course of the process can change along the way, but the desired result does not. To get to a desired process may require us to go left, right, above, below or through but we get to the result with a process.

By definition, "process" means **a series of actions or steps taken in order to achieve a particular end**. Now the curious part in the process definition is "particular end". What is the particular end? Does there need to be a particular end to a process or can it be a process with a particular "ongoing" or particular "development" or particular "direction"? I shared earlier about creating a process to get to a desired result and the definition of process speaks to a particular end. Then in the next sentence, I mention a particular ongoing, development or direction. A desired result, particular end and a particular ongoing, development and direction can co-exist in the same process. It sums up to basically getting to the next step, and not stopping when you make it to that step. This for me is what leadership has become.

Leadership is a process of visualizing the path, picturing the result, lighting up the path for others and staying locked on the ongoing, development and direction. A process of growing and serving. There is no end in leadership but a never-ending process of improvement, change, adapting, learning, and on and on. However, before a leader or anyone for that matter can create a process for which to lead themselves or others or to reach for a particular ongoing, development or direction, the most critical process to work on is a valuable three-step process. I have heard many times the statement "garbage in, garbage out". This is particularly true in all cases in life. What a person spends time immersed in, that will eventually fill their thoughts, their words and their movements.

I would imagine there could be multiple versions of the "garbage in, garbage out" statement if you consider it. How about, "mediocre in, mediocre out" or "average in, average out". Even still a better version could exist, "SUPERFANTASTIC in, SUPERFANTASTIC out". Bottom line, what you put in is what you get out of life and leadership. This is the process.

There is a valuable three-step process for me that supposes what you put in your mind, is what your thoughts become. What your thoughts become are the words you say. What your words say becomes the actions you take. I found this three-step process in my source for all guidance, the Bible. The SUPERFANTASTIC Process will stem from a simple yet immensely powerful statement from the Bible.

For out of the overflow of the heart the mouth speaks. The good man brings good things out of the good stored up in him. *Matthew 12:34-35*

In reviewing this powerful verse, what does Matthew mean by the overflow of the heart? The heart according to several scholars and sources refers to the inner person, their will and understanding, their character and their emotional nature. This verse is powerful to me as it presents the map for what we fill our mind, fills our heart which flows into our speech that in turn determines our actions. This to me speaks to a process. I love this simple process. This is the particular ongoing, development and direction. Fill the mind, speak your words from the mind and bring action from your spoken words. You will not speak or take action on things that are not in your mind. Conversely, you will speak and take action on the things that are in your mind.

But there is a bigger question from this process as well. How is the heart (or shall I say mind as another reference) filled so it can be overflowed? What makes us think the way we think?

What makes us speak the way we speak? What makes us act the way we act? We think, speak and act through which we fill our mind. We think by what we choose to allow to influence our behavior. Our mind is filled with what we allow to fill our mind, either by default or by design. What is the result of what we fill our mind? The things we fill up with become what we are focused on. This becomes what creates our persona or what others perceive as you. Or said in another way, what we fill our mind with is what is spoken from our mouth and acted upon when things get tough. How is it that we then speak what is in or on our mind? How do we speak to ourselves? We speak based on what we choose to fill our mind which then fills our heart. What is on our heart leads our voice. How is it that we act? We act based on what we filled our mind, spoken to our heart and ultimately drives our action.

This is the process that is the result of our think, speak and act. Good, bad or indifferent, it all stems from the process of filling our mind to our heart to our mouth. The incredible part of all of this is that it is our choice. You have the choice to determine what you will fill your mind, what you allow to be spoken out of your mouth and the actions you take. This is your choice to do it yourself or to give the control to someone else. No matter the world, the circumstance or surroundings, it is our choice to create a process to fill our mind, heart and voice with what we desire as the desired result, particular ongoing or direction.

There are two types of people in this world. Those that passively let the world fill their mind and those that choose what they will allow into their mind. If I can encourage you to be the latter, encourage you to choose the positive things to fill your mind, will you read this book? Will you make the decision that right now is the time in which you will make the change? A change that can alter your thinking process, alter your speech and alter your actions to move forward for the better.

There is no better time than the present moment... No better time than now to choose to live a life by design and create positive changes.

CONTENTS

INTRODUCTION

I have been fascinated with the leaders in my life. I have read about several leaders and have first-hand and second-hand experience with a multitude of leaders. Some leaders were thrust into the position and others slowly worked their way into it. My experiences with leaders have been positive and negative, but each has offered a lesson for me to learn. Even when I did not like it at the time, it was not until later in some instance that I realized what I needed to learn from that leader.

I have experienced leaders that positioned themselves as intelligent, simple, spiritual, angry, forceful, joyful and so many other ways. *I must admit, I have been a leader that has positioned myself in some positive and not so positive ways as well.* Each had a unique approach to their leadership. But it was their own unique process that created their own unique approach. Each filled my mind, heart and voice differently. It was my choice on how to process the lessons to get to my desired result, particular ongoing opportunity and ongoing result.

The SUPERFANTASTIC Process is an approach to guarding and choosing your sphere so that what fills your mind, influences what you think, to influence what you speak and to ultimately influence how you act. I bet you are a bit like me and wish there was a process to continually improve upon your leadership potential. A way in which you could positively impact your field or industry, the leader that others would seek out and follow. The type of leader that is absolutely successful in the pursuit of improving potential each and every day. There is… Let's begin down that yellow brick process road. And here is the first step…

WHAT DO YOU BELIEVE?
Just out of curiosity, answer the following questions:
- Do you believe you have greater potential?
- Do you believe you can become better today than you were yesterday?

- Do you believe you can become better tomorrow than you are today?
- Do you want to become a positive leader?

If you answer no to any of the questions above, ignore the no and act your way into the feeling as you go through the process. Stay with me as you press forward through your doubts and reservations. I believe you can and will answer yes to any one of these questions above if that is the choice you make. Answering no to any of the questions before speaks to you allowing outside influences to dictate what you think you can do. If you answered yes to any one of the questions above, then this book is for you and I am encouraging you to keep reading. Mike Rodriguez in _Finding Your Why_ points out, "All of us are capable of doing or achieving great things. So, the right question would be: Why don't we?"

Naturally, we want to be the best leader we can become. You have two options in your world: live a life by default or by design (explore more in-depth in my book _The SUPERFANTASTIC Principles_). A life by default gives up and goes passively with the circumstance. A life by design creates the circumstance and takes responsibility and personal accountability for each success and failure. The hard part is escaping the distractions of the world (tv, radio, social media, friends, etc.) that encourage a life by default. A life by design gives you the opportunity to dream and have visions of what you want your future to become. Yes, you can be that leader and realize your potential. I believe in you. Keith Craft in his book _Your Divine Fingerprint_ speaks to how everyone has 1% of uniqueness, a deposit of God's glory, that makes us special. Just imagine a leader that had the potential to positively impact many others in such a way that it created followable excellence for years to come. The methods and stories are closely discussed, studied and followed. The words and thoughts are quoted and repeated as the truth in leadership. Now there are amazing fans all over the world. The good news is that there is one such leader that existed in our world that created a pattern or process for us to follow so that we can become better through positive examples. His life, words and leadership examples are still debated, discussed and followed today even after so many years. Just one more thing, this leader never owned a business, only created one thing, never had any employees or made any money. This leader had a leadership style that was different from everyone at the time. This leader also had many haters, but the believers and followers ended up carrying on the leadership examples to change the world.

BIG PICTURE OF THE PROCESS

Let me share with you the setup of this book so that you can see and recognize the big picture as you go through the process. I believe that if you know the big picture before starting, it is easier to see why, how and what that the steps of the process fit and align along the way. This book is mainly set up in three sections. Identify, Investigate and Initiate. What does that mean and why is it set up like this? It is intentional to help you understand the process of growth.

I will share a quick analogy that was near and dear to me for several years. A long time ago I was over-weight and my health was spiraling out of control fast. Nothing was going to change for me until I found out why I needed to change. I identified that the pain of change (in my case creating a healthier lifestyle including better nutrition and exercise) was going to be less than the pain of not changing. From there I needed to investigate how to change. This was certainly a rough part of the process as it took some time to investigate the myriad of options out there. Then from embracing my why of change and the how to change, nothing was going to happen until I initiated the change. I had my process in place. Simple as that. It worked and worked incredibly well. This process is simple in its approach and practical in its application.

Identify

Investigate

Initiate

That's it. And now within this book, I will work with you to apply it to becoming a Positive THINK, SPEAK, ACT Leader. A process will never work until it's applied.

I have also included some bonus material to support you as you go through The SUPERFANTASTIC Process. This bonus material will provide you additional support and consideration too as you grow through what you are about to go through.

ARE YOU READY?

If I can share with you some of the wisdom, would you consider implementing it in your daily life and in your personal and work life? The SUPERFANTASTIC Process is the powerful steps taken in order for you to become a better leader for yourself and others. There is doubt in your mind at this point, I can tell. Lots of excuses and reasons are creeping into your mind as to why this is not plausible. STOP thinking why not. START thinking why not me and why not now. You already answered yes to one or more of the questions before, so you believe in yourself. STOP thinking you will do this later. If not now, when? When would be a good time to start? If you are waiting for the right moment, you will end up perpetually waiting.

Remember, you said yes. Yes, to your potential. To borrow from Mel Robbins in <u>The 5 Second Rule</u>, let's "5, 4, 3, 2, 1 – GO!" Keep reading. Let's start moving forward to a better tomorrow. The SUPERFANTASTIC Process is your way to identify, investigate and initiate your best positive Think, Speak, Act leadership. You can make incredible things happen for yourself and others.

Oh, I bet you are wondering who the leader is that I referenced earlier. Don't worry, I will share it later in the book.

For out of the overflow of the heart the mouth speaks.
The good man brings good things
out of the good stored up in him.

Matthew 12:34-35

The SUPERFANTASTIC Process

Chapter 1

Identify: POSITIVITY & LEADERSHIP

Would you be open-minded about changing, altering, adjusting your mindset about leadership in any capacity? Would you be open to viewing your perception, your filter, your current approach in which you view the world of leadership or your own leadership style? These are crucial questions to consider before you can move forward into The SUPERFANTASTIC Process.

In any conversation regarding change, it is imperative to start with why. Why are you making the change? This is the Identify part of the process. Once you identify why you are doing something it makes it easier. Let me share with you a quick story about how I was able to overcome a simple deep-rooted fear and do something I never thought I would be able to do.

I have always had an irrational fear of needles. I would stress and look away if I ever needed to get a shot from the doctor. I would grip the usual plastic seat cushion tight and look as far away as possible while the doctor gave me the shot. Giving blood was not a problem as long as I did not look at my arm during the process, like never. I would rather get a crick in my neck avoiding looking at the needle stuck in my arm than look anywhere near where the needle was in my arm. If I ever took my kids to get shots (thankful my wife would normally volunteer for that duty), I would hold my kid's hand, tell them all was ok, and we would look away together. I could tell that I was passing down my fear of shots to them.

Recently, my wife told me that due to a medical need, I would have to start giving her shots weekly. Wait... WHAT? I could feel the fear burning up through my body and my head began to feel woozy. Oh, and I forgot to mention when my wife got her epidural when having all four of our babies, I almost passed out all four times. Nevertheless, my wife assured me it

1

was necessary, and we had a doctor's appointment so the nurse could show me how to give my wife injections.

For days leading up to the appointment, including the drive to the office and walking into the doctor's office, I was convinced that I would not be able to do it. As much as I love my wife, the fear of needles and the thought of giving my wife a shot was never going to happen.

Standing in the doctor's room, the nurse came in and saw that I was visibly unnerved. At that point, the nurse and my wife began to explain the why. They identified for me the medical need and benefit for my wife to receive the injections weekly. Through my nerves and woozy head, I understood, and my perception of needles began to change. The nurse slowly instructed me through the process of preparing the syringe and injection site, cleaning the area and the required prep work. I realized suddenly, I was holding the needle in my hand and I was about to give my wife a shot under the supervision of the nurse. At that moment, I identified my why and understood this was important. Understanding it allowed me to prepare the area, and with much less trepidation, give my wife a shot. I'll be honest it is still not easy; I still get a little queasy, but I have my why, I understand I get to do this for my wife's health. My mindset changed. I have a new filter and perception of needles now. I have overcome a simple fear because I identified my why.

When you identify your why, it can be difficult. It can consist of staring down a fear or looking into something that is relatively unknown. Identifying it is where you lay the foundation of growth, success and overcoming fear. It is your path to be better.

I want to start this with something that you may find questionable. A phrase that at first glance you may take offense to. That is why I am going to say it to you. Read it out loud. Let it stew in your mind for a moment. Think about what I share before you continue reading on to the next paragraph.

I do not want you to become the best version of yourself.

Ok, now that you have read this out loud, stew on it. Some may even simmer on it and even some may have been offended; let it resonate within your mind and then let me explain. I mean no offense or disparaging comments from this statement. Why would I not want you to become the best version of you? The answer is simple: *potential improvement.* When you reach what you may perceive as perfection or the best version of yourself, then that is the moment in which you stop looking to grow and improve upon the why, how and what is your leadership skill set. The incredible thing about leadership is that it is ever-evolving. There should never be a moment that you stop looking to develop your skills. Personal development is a means and never an end to your growth. Becoming the best version of yourself should not be the desired result.

What I encourage you to do is to become a better version of yourself today than you were yesterday.

Believe you will be a better version of yourself tomorrow than you are today.

Potential improvement is a process each and every day, if you have faith in yourself. It is a leap of faith each day you wake up.

As I write these words, I am sitting on a bench while my son and his friend spend the next two hours jumping in a trampoline park and climbing through a myriad of obstacles both on the ground and elevated at least ten feet high above friends and family. In my view above my head at this moment is a young boy, no older than seven, strapped to a safety harness and rope is precariously traversing and with much trepidation through an obstacle about ten feet above the ground. As he struggles with shaky hands and a shaky voice to make his way to the next safe landing area, his fear is apparent and audible. His parents and family are cheering him on below. As he makes it past the first obstacle, he is relieved and shows a sense of calm that he has made it to the safe landing zone. He is done. However, in a few short moments, he realizes there is another obstacle in front of him to overcome in order to get to the next safe landing area. Through his parent's and family's encouragement, there is a greater sense of confidence that he can make it through the next obstacle and his positive outlook expands.

What a metaphor for our own leadership personal development. We may be fortunate enough to have a group of people cheering us on. We may have a safety rope to keep us safe in the event we slip or fall, and we even may have a safe landing zone to rest on as we overcome the current obstacle. However, if we do not have cheering crowds, the safety rope or a safe landing zone, we must still keep moving forward. Because if we do not keep moving forward then we become stuck on the one safe landing zone where we stopped. As we stop moving forward, our confidence and positive outlook will diminish along with potential growth.

I have been fortunate to make numerous mistakes and learn from each of them. Sometimes the same mistake more than once. Mistakes are part of our leadership personal development. Each mistake and success were a lesson learned and a growth opportunity. A valuable leader in my career shared that we will all make mistakes but to be mindful of the two different types. A misdemeanor and a felony mistake. The misdemeanors are the mistakes that can be overcome, can be fixed and are acceptable and encouraged to make (within reason). These are the risks that we take in order to see what will work and what will not work (you never know until you do; trying is simply an excuse to stop before it gets too hard). The felony mistakes are the ones in which we should know better than to make. These are the ones that are just against common sense and for a lack of better description, against the law. The only time you stop making mistakes is when you stop thinking, speaking and acting in any manner of growth. Essentially you are stuck, and things will begin to happen to you and not because of you.

There will be leadership obstacles to overcome, even some scary ones that we must traverse. When you feel you have become a perfect version of yourself it is only in the moment, it is when you arrived at the safe landing zone and stop moving forward. The future is where the leaders make their move, where they dare to think, speak and act in forward progression, leave their current safe zone to overcome the next obstacle knowing that it is potentially scary and unknown. As we keep moving forward our confidence grows, our development continues, and our understanding of leadership personal development improves. This is an ongoing, never-ending process if you are open to changing, altering, adjusting your mindset. I contend there is a process that you can adopt in which you are able to continue a positive approach to grow and develop your personal development of your leadership. A process that is systematic and helpful as you move forward off your safety zone and onto overcoming the next leadership obstacle.

As I was in the planning stage of writing this book, the title came to me pretty quickly and it felt right. On the heels of The SUPERFANTASTIC Principles, my notes for this book seemed to follow in order. If we are to lead, we should lead to the best of our abilities and spirit, but within an ordered approach. Leadership after all is an effort to orderly move people and or things positively forward.

The SUPERFANTASTIC Process was brought to life.

Why The SUPERFANTASTIC Process?

For me, SUPERFANTASTIC represents two things. I firmly believe there is a SUPER element or potential in each person. This is the gifting or talent that we have all been blessed with. The struggle for some is finding this super inside. A lot of people will look to find their super from the outside in as opposed to the inside out. The SUPER is inside and needs to be found there. Once you find and apply your super, that is when you can create the FANTASTIC around you. The title in itself is a process. First, identify, investigate, initiate the super, what you have inside you. Then identify, investigate, initiate a fantastic, the environment or circumstance around you. See, super you, then fantastic around you. Super inside, Fantastic outside.

The next question I hope you ask in reference to this book and what The SUPERFANTASTIC Process is what's in this for me? I am glad you are asking this question (even if prompted a little). Why would you spend time reading this book and Why The SUPERFANTASTIC Process specifically? My goal here is to help you. Make you uncomfortable. Make you check yourself. I started this message with a question already and will continue to ask more from you throughout this book.

This book may not be for you, I get it. You may not want to "answer" or "participate" in the questions and actions within this book. If you don't, then you are only cheating yourself and missing an opportunity to grow through a process, The SUPERFANTASTIC Process. Stay committed with me through this book. The only thing you may gain is elevating your approach as a positive leader. What do you have to lose? Stay the same or risk getting better.

The SUPERFANTASTIC Process is just that, a process. Intentions to improve will only get you thinking about the safe landing zone of your obstacle course. The process will get you to the actual obstacle of growth and improvement to become a Positive Leader with a Think, Speak, Act process. If you want to traverse the obstacles of a positive leader, then step off the safe landing zone. Encourage yourself to step through the first obstacle, train yourself to overcome the hurdles and obstacles along the way. The process prepares you for it. Here is your training manual.

Before you can become a positive leader and continue to engage your leadership personal development, I would present to you for consideration the importance to Think as a Positive Leader, Speak as a Positive Leader and Act as a Positive Leader. You must think it to speak it and then speak it to act it. Or simply put, you must speak what you think so you can do what you say.

Now within The SUPERFANTASTIC Process, two powerful components need to be explained: Positivity and Leadership. These two concepts will be your umbrella over the process by which you Think, Speak and Act. Without positivity and leadership, then your Think, Speak and Act will be without context. This context guides and influences the process.

Within the process of Think, Speak and Act as a positive leader, it is important to know what these two components mean and apply them. Why they are so important to the process. Without these two components of positivity and leadership, the

Think, Speak and Act are simply just that, concepts. There becomes no value within the process as these concepts layer within each other.

Here you can break the leadership curse you may have experienced or are currently experiencing. Here is your opportunity to create a legacy of leadership that can extend beyond you. Your awareness or ability to identify your opportunity is the first step in the process of making positive changes and tackling your next leadership obstacle with confidence. Let me ask you a tough question right now. For this to work, I need you to be honest with yourself.

What is your predisposed manner when faced with difficulty or change as a leader?

If you are a bit like me, then I imagine most of us would lean to a negative manner when faced with a difficulty. Biologically we are wired towards a negative bias. Our minds look for the negativity in any situation. It is an innate defense response. It's just who we are as humans. As humans, we are gifted (or cursed depending on how you look at it) to find the negativity in most situations as part of our instinct to survive. And our instinct to survive has changed over time as the perceived dangers change. The good news from this is that you can re-train your brain. You can re-wire your filter, your pre-disposition or instinct of negativity in order to focus on positive opportunities with any changes you experience. Survival mode can be adjusted, tweaked if you will, in order to change from a fight or flight response to a "can do" and "will do" response.

Why is it important to identify your pre-disposed survival mode (fight or flight) manner when faced with change as a leader? Because when you initiate your manner (or SUPER), your team is watching and modeling your behavior. What you initiate becomes what others follow. What you initiate either endears your team to you and the goal or pushes them away from you and the goal. Now that you have identified your pre-disposed manner in challenging circumstances, what do you do with that knowledge? Here and now I am challenging you to make a change for the better. Make a choice and take action to replace your negative pre-disposition with positivity and leadership.

POSITIVITY!

Let's further identify the components of positive. Now, I am not talking about the skipping around chasing rainbows and unicorns' type of positivity. My intent with identifying and discussing positivity is to create an understanding of a new perspective, a new filter and a new mindset. The kind of positivity that recognizes the negative, the obstacles and the hurdles and still does something constructive with it. This is a mindset that creates a new filter that you see the world, people, places, things and most importantly, opportunities. Without a positive component then the world is simply a mess of chaos, people are potential trouble, places are a wreck, things are a distraction and opportunities are no more than problems that cannot be overcome. So, what is the positive component? Let's start with a definition.

Positive – definition: *consisting of or characterized by the presence or possession of features or qualities rather than their absence. Constructive, optimistic or confident. Good or useful.*

Now that we have identified what positive is, let's identify why positivity is so important.

Why should you have positivity?

The Mayo Clinic describes several health benefits of being positive including increased life span, lower rates of depression, lower levels of distress, better psychological and physical well-being and most importantly as a leader, better coping skill during hardship and times of stress. This alone should be enough of a reason to start skipping down the sidewalk or office hallway and whistling a happy tune every   day. So, if amazing health benefits of positivity are not enough, then what will persuade us to have positivity?

Let's identify the benefits of this a little more, the definition of the word positive, notes presence or possession of… rather than the absence. So how do you obtain this presence or possession of positivity? Choice and action.

Positivity is merely a construct in our own minds. It is only a series of thoughts and perceptions in your own mind that you have chosen to think in order to feel a certain way. I'll be honest with you, when you see things in a positive manner, the world around you does not change. The chaos, people, trouble, wrecks and distractions do not magically disappear. On the contrary, the only thing positivity does is change the way you see and perceive these things of the world.

Even though positivity is a mere construct in our own minds, it still takes choice and action to create this construct. A designed approach to have "possession of" rather than the "absence of" positivity. If you do not take possession of your thoughts and take possession of positivity, then something else will fill the void. Your default mind will revert to its instinctive negative bias. Negativity loves to fill the vacuum created by default thinking.

Take hold of positivity. Make the choice and take the action to take possession of positivity. There is plenty of positivity to go around, grab yours. Better yet, it is free and abundant. When you can look to see things in a positive manner, you are able to hear things in a positive manner. This opportunity is not only for you but for other people you encounter.

How can you identify the practical and strategic advantage of positivity? This is relatively easy. When there is a positive filter, the opportunity within a problem, roadblock or hurdle will be easier to find. Without the positivity filter, it becomes easier to give up when the problem, roadblock or hurdle presents itself. The mistakes become catastrophic and fixes become limited or non-existent. I understand this sounds soft with respect to being practical or strategic. So, I ask you to look at it another way. Here are a few real-life examples to consider.

You are driving your car and along the way and the engine light comes on. The car is still driving well, but the engine light is still on taunting you from the dashboard. You have numerous options to deal with this perceived problem. Put tape over the light pretending the problem does not exist and hope it goes away, but we all know how that will end. This is your default approach. You could get angry because you are always spending money on your car. After all, it is terrible, and you should sell it and get a new car. The anger will not solve the problem though. It will only prolong it and cause you frustration. This is a negative approach. Or you can get to an auto repair shop quickly to have an expert check it out to identify the problem. Yes, the fix could be expensive, or the fix could be relatively cheap. However, at least you have identified the "why" to give you the opportunity to investigate and initiate a reasonable solution. This is your positive approach.

Another example: you look at your current job or position. You made a mistake that will cause some issues for you and potentially some other people. Again, you have numerous options to address this identified mistake. First, you could stress about it and try to hide the mistake and hope no one finds out. This is your default approach plus an extra sign for making bad choices. Another option is to get angry, try to figure out who you could outright blame or deflect the accountability. You could rant that you were under pressure and that you don't have the right tools to do your job or a series of other excuses. This is deflecting responsibility. As you can imagine, excuses are just another way of saying a negative approach. Finally, your best option would be to identify the mistake, identify how it happened, identify how to prevent it from happening again and make the fix. Share your results with your team and you will have not only fixed an error you made, but you will also have added value to the team and organization. You created an opportunity to support other team members and protect the organization from duplicating a mistake. This is your classic and most valuable positive approach.

So, if positivity is a mere construct in our mind and there are practical and strategic advantages to being positive, the next question is, how can I become positive? This is a two-step process. First is identifying the negative so that you can remove it or reframe it and then immediately replace it with positivity. If you remove something, it is important to intentionally replace it with something better. If not, by default, the previous negative thinking will return to fill the vacuum.

A Mayo Clinic article titled "Positive Thinking: Stop negative self-talk to reduce stress" presented some steps in order to work on clean up the negativity and replace it with positivity.

- Identifying negative thinking includes recognizing your filtering, personalizing, catastrophizing and polarizing of thoughts.

- Identifying positive thinking includes identifying areas to change, checking yourself, being open to humor, following a healthy lifestyle, surrounding yourself with positive people and practicing positive self-talk.

Let's look at some examples of replacing a negative thought with a positive thought. Your thoughts are simply your approach to how you view things, opportunities and obstacles.

Negative Approach	Positive Approach
I'm busy	I will make time
I can't do it	I can do it
Fake it until I make it	Faith it until I make it
Not sure if...	I got this...
Looks good but...	Looks good and...
I would do this but...	I will do this and...
I am just a [insert job title]	I am the [insert job title]

A negative approach can be replaced with a positive approach. A negative approach allows us to "hedge your bets". So often the negative approach is just that: a way to guard ourselves against hurt, failure or embarrassment. Within the list is a phrase that has always created a strong impression for me. You will find it said on fun little quotes to "fake it until you make it." I placed it in the negative approach. Why? Well, "fake it until you make it" is allowing for an excuse to not complete your goal. You are simply pretending to do something, there is no belief in yourself in the statement. However, if you adjust it to "Faith it until I make it" there includes a factor of belief. The word faith inserts itself in the statement as an assertion of belief. When you believe it, you can and will do it (whatever it may be). The positive approach is a commitment to yourself. It is a commitment to others. It is a commitment to creating a mindset of opportunities through positivity. Review the phrases we shared in the paragraph before.

Now, let's continue with identifying our positive approach. Will you fail sometimes with a positive approach? ABSOLUTELY! You will also learn a great deal with a positive approach. The positive approach recognizes that failure is part of this process. Failure can be turned into the most valuable lessons. A negative approach will prevent you from getting to the valuable lessons and growth. What is it about a positive approach that is so impactful? For this answer, I found a person that certainly lives, breathes and walks the talk of a positive approach. When you are focused on something you will find it.

I discovered just that person while conducting research in this area. In this discussion I will simply call him Coach. During the course of writing this book, I had been researching positivity to offer additional insight on how to think, speak and act positively. In my search for someone that exhibits the traits of positivity, I was immediately drawn to Coach. Coach was a person that I accidentally discovered on LinkedIn. I encountered one of his articles and was instantly intrigued. From that one article Coach artfully articulated in such few words the impact of a positive approach. Not just any type of positive approach, but an authentic positive approach. From that moment, I began to follow Coach on LinkedIn.

Every day, sometimes several times a day, I found Coach sharing insights on his perception of what an authentic positive approach means in all types of situations. This guy was speaking my language. He got it and was not only applying it in his personal life but in his professional life as well. His approach also presented a way to apply it to your own world.

Within a short while, I was eager to consume his words on LinkedIn, his Facebook group and ultimately daily positive texts. I knew I needed to connect with Coach. Through messages and texts, I was able to finally connect with him. I reached out to Coach while writing this book specifically to ask some questions about his authentic positive approach. During our conversation, he shared his powerful story and the people he encountered that allowed him to re-think and re-examine his approach. He created an authentic positive mindset from his encounters and experiences to help himself and others.

Coach spoke with me at length and was seemingly eager to connect with a fellow positive person and one that was intrigued by his approach. During our phone conversation, I was able to ask Coach a series of questions regarding positivity. On the phone, I could tell Coach Fred was smiling as I asked my series of questions. His enthusiasm for life, for helping others and watching it multiply was contagious. As we concluded our call, I felt inspired by Coach's excitement for being authentic and positive. And that is the point of positivity. When you focus on a positive perspective, you will find positive opportunities no matter if you succeed or fail. When you share positivity it becomes contagious, even over the phone. For positivity to be a filter, or perspective rather, it has to become an intentional choice.

How is it that we talk about positive and positivity in relation to action, and making a specific choice? Well, I am glad you are asking all these great questions along the way. Let's talk about our emotions. Ok, not the mushy type of emotional talk, but the kind of talk that references emotion as a verb. The word emotion is traditionally defined as a noun. However, in my book (literally), it is now a verb as it is modified slightly. Is positive an emotion? Yes, it is, as defined as so in the dictionary. But what if we identify what emotions do for us. It sets things in motion. So here and now we will officially add a modification to the word emotion to become "E-Motion". Let's really dig into what it can do for us. Let me explain.

E-Motion

Emotion is defined in the dictionary as a natural instinctive state of mind deriving from one's circumstance, mood, or relationship with others. Do you realize that in the dictionary, emotion is basically defining it as being affected by our environment? You are being controlled by the things or people around you. That is an outside-in approach. But let's look at emotion or e-motion as an inside-out approach.

Which option do you think will become more productive: acting your way into a feeling or feeling your way into an action? Not sure on this one yet? Let me give you an example. How many of you have felt like exercising and then started exercising or how many of you started exercising and then felt better? Trust me, when I was on a competitive triathlon team there were many instances in which I had to act my way into a feeling, over feeling my way into action to train for races. Or even still, there were times I did not feel like working on a project for work but knowing it was necessary, I acted my way into the feeling of accomplishment. So, if we adopt e-motion as our new modified definition, then we begin to act our way into a feeling. Here is our proposed definition of e-motion.

E-motion can be defined as a chosen state of mind creating one's circumstance, mood, or relationship with others.

Do you see the difference? You change your noun to a verb with a few carefully placed words and it will make all the difference. "Chosen" and "creating" make all the difference in the definition. This is an internal choice and does not depend on external factors. But how does this apply to positivity? This is where you chose positive as your e-motion. Because the alternative is to choose negative or pessimistic as your e-motion.

A positive e-motion is a choice to create your circumstance, mood and relationship with others, with a positive filter. You incorporate joy, gratitude, serenity, interest, hope, pride, amusement, inspiration, awe and love into your thoughts, speech and actions. Your positive e-motion is your new filter in which you interact with the world. Now, I am sure there is still an internal struggle to validate having a positive e-motion over being realistic. How do you overcome this? Well, being realistic is accepting of how things are now and accepting the perceived truth about life. An "it is what it is" mindset. Feels like a default approach if you ask me. And that is fine. However, if you leave it there then you miss the future opportunity. A positive e-motion does not discount the here and now, it recognizes the here and now and the perceived truth of life and it adds a layer on top of it that creates a movement of action to create a positive circumstance, mood or relationship. Positive e-motion is what you chose to add, to layer on to the here and now.

Positive e-motion can also be viewed as a tool. Something that you use to get to the next level. Only accepting how and where things are will stall you out. Effectively using a tool such as positive e-motion will allow you to find opportunities to improve. What you focus on is what you will find. Positive e-motion is your currency to spend on opportunity. The question is: How will you spend it? Where will you invest it? What is your interest rate? What is your ROI with your positive e-motion? Let's continue to build our foundation. What happens next is we need to continue to layer on identifying our next conversation points. After positivity, we need to move to leadership.

LEADERSHIP!

Now that we have identified positive, let's identify the second part of this conversation: Leadership. In our view of leadership, we see many different versions of this word. Many come from our first had experiences, maybe a current boss, a boss that you had at some point in time in your career, a leader that inspired you or a leader that frustrated you. We even have views of leaders that our friends and colleagues talk about or the ones we see on the screen from tv shows or movies. The potential list of leaders in our sphere is almost inexhaustible. No wonder we struggle with our filter and view of what a leader should be and how we should model our own behavior as a leader.

Leadership – definition: *the action of leading a group of people or an organization.*

This is a solid definition of leadership. I wholeheartedly believe there is another valuable definition of leadership. Leadership can include leading one person. And that one person is yourself. This is a critical part of leadership in my view. It is not necessary for you to be a person in charge of tens or hundreds or thousands of people to be a leader. If you lead yourself well and become a light for others to follow and emulate, then you are without a doubt a shining example (pun intended) of leadership.

For me, for leadership to be wholly defined there are certainly more types of leadership. I would even expand on this definition to share there are <u>two</u> types of leadership that create a resulting type of leadership. The types must go in proper order for the third type of leadership to be realized. The two types of leadership are in this order: Internal Leadership and External Leadership. When these two are addressed properly, then you result in Overall Leadership. This formula is a process.

Internal Leadership plus External Leadership creates Overall Leadership

And the process repeats and repeats and repeats. You cannot have a complete formula of leadership without a complete process. Let me clarify a little in reference to the internal-leadership plus external-leadership, which creates overall-leadership. In the next chapter, we will investigate how the combination of positivity and leadership goes, so I will not dive deep into it here. However, with that being said, earlier we identified positivity. As we start identifying leadership, we can begin using positivity as a filter in which you view leadership. Without the right filter, leadership can be taken in the wrong direction very quickly. So where do we start? Most importantly, why is this important? Let's start with a discussion about honor. Honor is the foundation of successful internal, external and overall leadership. Let's talk a little about honor, what it is and what it means. When you boil it down, honor is simply respect. This is the WD-40 by which leadership is kept running smoothly. It is the relationship lubricant that keeps the connections from getting stuck or breaking down. Leadership in any capacity is about building and maintaining relationships. For without successful relationships, there is little that can be accomplished. You will find honor is critical in all aspects of internal, external and overall leadership. Let's review each component of the leadership formula.

Internal Leadership (Honor Self)

Why would we consider internal leadership when the definition of leadership makes no mention of this?   My first leadership question for you is, who do you think you are leading first? Even though the official definition of leadership indicates an action of leading a group of people or an organization, I feel it is important to provide leadership for yourself first. If you say you are leading other people before leading yourself, then you are jumping the gun. You are putting the cart before the horse. This is the first step in the process: Internal Leadership. If you think you can lead others and not lead yourself first, then you are fooling yourself and no one else will believe in you as a leader. Internal leadership is the care and maintenance you provide to yourself so that you can eventually lead others. This is where you recognize that honoring yourself is important. When you fail to honor yourself, you lose sight of what makes you important. It is the example you set that others can build trust.

Consider these examples of people in positions that fail to honor themselves and create internal leadership. They could all possibly do their job or task, but would you have their trust as a leader? As a school bus driver, their job is to safely drive a group of students to school. However, before the school bus driver can drive a group of students to school, the driver must complete numerous steps and training to even become a school bus driver. Along with all the steps and training to become a school bus driver, they must drive well even if they are not driving students around.   If you saw your child's school bus driver on the road and they were driving erratically or worse yet, drinking and driving, would you ever allow your child on that school bus again with that driver? I imagine not.

Another example: a fitness trainer's job is to support people to make better health choices including food-related choices and physical exercise. The fitness trainer must also take steps to know about food choices and all the things associated with physical exercise. It is their job to understand and help their clients execute the plan to improve their health. If you saw your fitness trainer at every fast food restaurant with empty bags and wrappers of unhealthy food and never exercising, it would be very difficult to follow your fitness trainer's instructions when they are not able to follow their own leadership. Yet a more common example to review would be a team leader.

A team leader's job is to support a team to reach organizational goals.   The team leader does this through scheduling, directing and planning out tasks, projects and actions, so that the team can accomplish their goals to ultimately accomplish the organizational goals.   If the team leader is so focused on organizational goals that the human goals become collateral damage, then it becomes difficult to follow and believe in the team leader.   If the team leader is unable to handle stress, lashes out at team members at the slightest error or overcome obstacles and hurdles both personally and professionally, then the team leader is lacking internal leadership.

In the three examples noted before, these individuals (the school bus driver, the fitness trainer and the team leader) have a responsibility to exhibit a thinking, speaking or acting approach that is consistent with their role and what their influence means, even if perceived, for others.   If there is a deviation from why you do the things you do, others will notice. To lead yourself and to lead yourself well, it is critical to identify the why you do the things you do.   As a school bus driver should not drink and drive at any time, a fitness trainer should be mindful of their own personal fitness and nutrition goals and a team leader should be able to handle their own personal goals and setbacks.   In any role, you should live a life in which others can admire, and or follow.   Giving honor to yourself first allows a person to adhere to what is right and maintain a standard of conduct.

Internal leadership is the process by which you lead yourself. How is this accomplished? It's relatively simple. Here is where, as a self-leader, you start developing internal leadership. It does not happen in a vacuum. When you fill your mind, you will then speak what you know and can act on what you speak. See, this is the keystone by which internal leadership develops. The good person brings out good things, out of the good stored up. We can rephrase the statement even more. A good leader brings out good leadership, out of the good leadership stored up inside.

Internal leadership is the act of storing up good leadership examples within. What you honor for yourself, you can honor for others. When you are filled with internal leadership development and honor, then your team will reap the benefits. We will explore what it means to initiate filling your mind in the THINK chapters of this book.

External Leadership (Honor Others)

Now is the time to factor in the next step of the process: External Leadership. Why would you consider external leadership separately from internal leadership? Well, internal leadership is the process in which you honor yourself to address your own path. External leadership is the process in which you give honor to others to support their path or goals.

I am sure you are thinking, what does honor have to do with leading others? Why should I give honor to my team that gets paid to work, to do a job or complete tasks? Didn't they sign up for this job and isn't it the leader's job to make sure they do it? I get paid to make sure they do their job and if I become all soft, then I risk losing my job when the team does not do their job. These are certainly fine questions to ask and consider. They are indeed valid. Yes, people did sign up for the job. Yes, the leader's job is to ensure the team is all headed in the defined direction and completing their defined job or tasks appropriately. However, I would add the following, could you lead a team with your examples of internal leadership to be more?

It's easy to lead team members that are compliant, helpful, supportive and nice. I would contend that almost any reasonable leader could lead a team that is in good condition. Giving honor to those that honor you in your role, title or position is simple and easy. However, if faced with a team that is non-compliant, destructive, fighting and or downright mean, or in a challenging environment, then only a leader that has developed internal leadership can make a positive difference. Giving honor to those that dis-honor you, your role or position and even the job they have been trusted with is the greatest gift of leadership.

I have walked into teams that have been both compliant and stubborn. One of my most memorable situations of creating external leadership stemmed from coming into a team as the leader behind a previously less than honorable leader. The team had little trust and awareness of their own opportunity. Over time, patience and by gaining trust through setting the example and expectations, the team eventually came around and eventually showed their potential.

External leadership is the opportunity you have as a leader to share the honor you have stored up in yourself from honoring yourself. Being an example to your team and giving honor will lead your team to begin storing up the honor you give to them. The next step of leadership will organically start occurring as you begin duplicating the leadership in your team and the honor that is layered within this process.

Overall Leadership (Duplicate Honor)

Identifying why it is important to develop internal leadership and external leadership will lead you ultimately to Overall Leadership. When you reach this stage then you have opportunities to duplicate all the efforts for yourself and others. In some business settings, this is where you would hear about scaling your product.

Is creating additional leaders and honor a product? I would certainly say you could see it as that. Would scaling or duplicating your product help improve not only your team but your organization as well? Yes, and yes. The more leaders, the more honor you have within an organization, the more opportunities for growth will occur. Getting to this point is not easy. You may not reach all team members at once at this stage. You may find some team members will catch on to the process quicker than others.

As you start finding team members catching on and displaying internal and external leadership, support those team members to support others through the process. This is where more of your team starts to recognize through examples of why internal leadership is valuable and the why external leadership is effective. Here you not only create more leaders, but you also create more honor among your team. When honor is abundant, honor will multiply. As mentioned before, multiplying your product or scaling up can be beneficial.

Why is this important to follow the process to obtain overall leadership? Here is my perspective. I strongly believe that a sign of a strong positive leader is how well a team performs when the leader is not present. If your team can function and function well without a leader, then you have a team that has some if not several other leaders within the overall-leadership sphere. If as a leader when you leave your team alone, they are constantly calling you or things begin to fall apart, then that is a tell-tale sign you have the opportunity to help grow your team through internal and external leadership.

One more sign of creating an overall leader on your team, they get promoted appropriately or you recognize that team member(s) could eventually easily replace you in your job. This can certainly be unnerving for some leaders, at the thought of your team coming for your job but look at it another way. If you are the type of leader that can create additional leaders that get promoted or that could fill your position, then you are the type of leader that will be recognized and will more than likely have more opportunities than you can imagine.

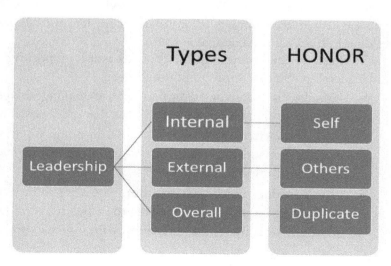

Why are we spending so much time simply identifying what for most are common concepts? Why would we consider devoting the beginning of this book to this? I cannot stress enough that building your foundation is critical. When you build a foundation on sand, your entire structure, perception, approach will crumble during the first storm you attempt to weather. If you spend time to build a strong foundation, understanding and recognizing why you have certain perceptions and filters of positivity and leadership, then you will certainly weather the storms as they come. And those storms will come.

Character Foundation

Let me provide one more set of conversations to identify a valuable component of positivity and leadership. This will be your character. Whatever foundation you build will eventually show your character. Identifying your character is important but understanding why you have the character you have is equally important. Earlier I asked what your demeanor is when faced with a difficulty. This is a telling question. Most people can fake a character in good times. In bad times most people will expose their true character. So why am I asking you to recognize your true character here? Because again, the character in partnership with internal leadership is the foundation you will stand on when things are good and bad. What you are filled with is what will spill when you are bumped. It's not the cup, it's not who is holding it, it's what's inside that is spilled.

Let's review some general characteristics of positivity and leadership you can stand on in tough times.

- Humility is generally identified as not making things about you. That there are other ideas that quite possibly could be better than your own. Admitting when a mistake is made and being grateful for other's influence and contribution towards success.
- Obedient does not necessarily mean you are submissive to another, but that you are willing to respectfully follow a request or support the direction of the organizational goals.

- Clarity allows for being transparent, and coherent to your thoughts and core values. Your vision towards a goal is not swayed by external momentary influence.

- A Team builder is the one that will strive to support and grow the team in good times and bad. There is a protective instinct to have your team's "back" when things get tough.

- Relationships are how leaders know and understand others. It is how teams are connected that binds them together especially in the tough times.

- Engaged is the occupied focus obtained for the person, place or thing. This is the process by which you develop relationships with others.

- Disciplined is the ability to control behavior or the way of working. Consistently working to the accepted goal.

- Empower is giving away authority. Instilling confidence in others to do more, be more and create more. Letting go of your control so others can explore their leadership opportunities.

Identifying why Positivity and Leadership are so important is a critical step in this process. Before you move onto the next chapter, spend some time reflecting on why any of these conversations resonate with you. Why you see positivity and leadership the way you do. Getting your why right, is your foundation. Getting the why of your positivity and leadership understanding and perspective will allow you to build and layer the additional steps within this book. Below are some tasks to complete in order to work on and internalize your why. Spend time working on these assignments. Then after some time, I ask you to return to your why and see how you have grown through the process of applying all the steps within this process.

Identify: Positivity & Leadership *Wrapped Up*

Open-Minded	Evaluate why you are the way you are.
The SUPERFANTASTIC Process	The process through which you build you so you can build others and your environment.
Positivity	Understand the benefits of embracing positivity.
Approach	Recognize two distinct approaches that produce one distinct result.
E-Motion	Chosen state of mind.
Leadership	Understand there are additional components to the definition.
Internal-Leadership	Honoring yourself.
External-Leadership	Honoring others.
Overall-Leadership	Duplicating honor.
Character	What is displayed during tough times?

ACTION & STEPS: Process Planning Notes

Question	Your Thoughts
Identify why you perceive / filter "Positivity and Leadership" the way you do?	
Investigate how you would elevate your "Positivity and Leadership" approach?	

Initiate what would be your "Positivity and Leadership" approach?	
Additional Considerations	

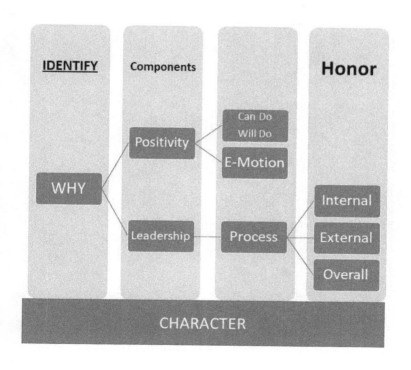

Chapter 1   Identify: POSITIVITY & LEADERSHIP

Chapter 2

Investigate: POSITIVE LEADERSHIP

Congrats! In most real-world applications of leadership, most people would skip the Identify part and jump right into the how-to-do something. Few will develop their why before attempting to be a leader. Even more, will jump right into the action or initiate part of the process before building the foundation or investigating how to be an effective leader. At this point, you are already elevated above most because you have spent time identifying your why. This is your foundation on which you will build on. What happens next is, we will investigate the how of positive leadership. This is where we will work on your filter or perceptions of positive leaders. Let's peek behind the filters and perceptions and investigate how you see the way you see and how to work through the process of adjusting your filters.

How do you know about positive leadership now? How have you filled your mind, heart and voice based on your experiences, circumstances and surroundings? How you think about positive leadership is based on how you were taught to think about or experienced leadership. Can you at this moment consider there could be a different view on positive leadership than what you know and filter through your current vision?

Remember, what you fill your mind with determines your speech and guides your action. How you determine the source of your process, the filter by which you perceive your circumstance and environment will determine your process to initiate. Even your current "think" went through a process to get where it is now. So, could there have been a process in which you created your perception of positivity and leadership? Could there have been a process in which you think, speak and ultimately act as a leader? Could it be possible there are different views, thoughts on positive leadership?

Tom Rath in his article "The Impact of Positive Leadership" in Gallup News shares that "What differentiates positive leaders from the rest? Instead of being concerned with what they can *get out of* their employees, positive leaders search for opportunities to *invest in* everyone who works for them." My next question is how do you do this? How do you investigate creating your process to invest in yourself and others as a positive leader? We will bank on this process shortly.

Positive Psychology in their article titled "Positive Leadership: 30 Must-Have Traits and Skills" speaks to positive leadership as deviant – positively deviant. "Being positively deviant (leadership) means that the style, technique or behavior the leader engages falls outside the normal range observed in leadership." WHAT? This is a strong statement sharing that positive leadership is not normal and it falls outside the social norms of leadership. Isn't it scary to fall out of social norms and to be different? Not if you have a firm foundation of why you are a positive leader.

Using the word deviant to describe positive leadership creates such a strong picture of what would be considered abnormal. This description crashes hard on the impact of our normal experience with leadership. Positive leadership would be considered so far out of the standard range or social norm, that it would necessitate the word deviant. How do you perform positive leadership if it is so abnormal or deviant? We discussed earlier the approach to leadership with a process or formula if you will. Be proud to be considered abnormal or positively deviant. Nothing normal ever truly changed the lives of others into something so much more. If you want to be extra or different or abnormal or even deviant, become a positive leader. There is a process for this.

I would ask you to combine this process formula to start honoring yourself, honor others and then watch your honor duplicate, multiply and grow. How you become positively deviant is through standing on your why foundation and filtering it through the components of leadership.

Internal Leadership plus External Leadership creates Overall Leadership

Let's navigate options for how to plan your positive leadership formula. We know why this formula is so important, so let's explore the approach for how to make it happen.

Internal

How do you create a plan for internal leadership?

Planning how you will start developing internal leadership is an important part of the process. I do want to insert that the world does not stop as you are planning to better yourself by creating a plan for internal leadership. This process is a progression that will grow and improve over time as you plan and then put into action. Be prepared because you will fail along the way. However, having a plan will get you to the goal fast than jumping into the action part. Let's start with what it means to plan for internal leadership.

Part of the how involves internalizing the plan so that it is part of your daily routine. Internalize what the plan is so that you fill your mind with it. At that point, it is not about remembering what you planned, it is becoming what you planned. Let's talk through some steps to creating a plan. Start reading more (this book is a great example), start listening to positive leadership examples and align yourself with positive leaders that you would like to emulate. Surround yourself with the examples that can help you positively grow. Only by filling yourself with positive leadership examples and knowledge can you overflow and light the path for others. Let's continue to investigate the how of building and growing your internal leadership development.

Alignments are your connections that will make a positive difference in your life. One point of consideration is making sure you pick the right alignments. Ones that will support you when they recognize you are going off the trail. These are the people that will encourage you to think better, speak kinder and act with intention. The right alignments are the ones you can call at 2am to discuss a problem or an idea. As important as having the right alignments are in your life, it is just as critical to be the right alignment for someone else as well.

Mentors can be the next level in developing your internal leadership. A wise man will always seek wise counsel. In most cases, mentors will cost money. Consider it an investment in you, your future, your potential and your future earning potential. There is a return on investment with a mentor if you apply it well. The minute you recognize that you cannot grow in a vacuum and need the support and guidance of a mentor, is the moment you will start expanding your boundaries. Mentors can help you see things from a different perspective; see things that you would have otherwise never considered. A solid mentor will encourage you to review and understand why you think the way you think. Having a mentor is literally eye-opening in many cases. A recent example from a conversation with my mentor Mike Rodriguez, included him having me read a chapter in his book again. This time, he asked me to simply insert my name throughout the chapter in place of the word prospect. This simple change, this simple shift in perspective was an eye-opening event. We spoke for over an hour discussing this change of perspective and how impactful it was. That is the kind of power a mentor can have in your life.

Read or listen to books that fill your mind with the type of information that will be beneficial to you. If you want to grow your strengths, then find books that discuss your strengths. If you want to work on your weakness, then find books that complement what you are looking to improve. The time you spend with a book is an investment again in you, your future, your potential, and your future earning potential. There are so many books out there to choose from to support you in your goal (this one included). Find the ones that spark your interest. Get recommendations from your mentors or other individuals that you admire. Start a library of books you read as a reference for later. Highlight the best concepts and quotes that you will use and apply from the book. As crazy as it sounds, if you read a book that positively impacts you, reach out to the author. Send a message, email, LinkedIn message, Facebook message, Instagram or even snail mail to the author. Thank them for the book and the information. I promise you, more times than not, you will get a reply from the author (this one included). You will be surprised how meaningful it is to an author to hear from a reader. You never know, it may turn into an alignment or mentor opportunity.

Watch what will help you grow. All too often we spend time drowning ourselves in movies, tv, social media that will do nothing for us except temporarily entertain us or numb our brains. Don't get me wrong, there is nothing wrong with making time for entertainment, but remember your time is your currency. How will you spend it? If you can make time for entertainment, you can make time for growth. Another investment potential in you. Be mindful of the sources of your information. You will find some sources that are ideological and some that are pragmatic and others that are a mix of the two. Understanding the difference will help you when you process what you have viewed. Every bit of video is produced through a video lens as well as the person's lens or perspective of that topic. It is important for you to research and develop your own perspective on the information you view.

Learn at every opportunity. Yes, reading books, listening to podcasts, joining educational webinars, going to classes, and more are excellent opportunities to learn. I unequivocally recommend searching out these types of structured and organized learning opportunities whenever and wherever you can. Some are free and some cost money. Again, these are investments in your future potential. The potential values from these are important. The other just as important learning opportunities come from your mistakes and other's mistakes. We will all have plenty of mistakes along the way to learn from if you recognize the mistake and the lesson contained within it. Do not dismiss a mistake at face value. Truly review and investigate how the mistake occurred and how you can improve moving forward. All moments in life are learning opportunities, if you investigate them. This is certainly not an exhaustive list of ways to investigate how to develop your internal leadership. How you proceed through your internal leadership growth is personal and unique. We may all start down one path and identify that there are other options and start investigating how to implement a new internal leadership growth path. What it should all have in common is that you are investigating how to grow yourself and honor yourself through the development of your thoughts, speech and actions. Once you begin to internalize your plan for internal leadership, then you are ready to begin the next step into external leadership.

External
How do you create a plan for external leadership?

Let me explain some examples of honoring others through external leadership. Here are the opportunities to use honor as your guide. Consider these examples of giving honor to others through external leadership.

Correct and redirect timely is a way in which you can honor your team as a leader. When a team member begins to make poor choices or steer away from the goal of the organization or team, it is the leader's responsibility to correct the behavior or action and redirect in a timely fashion. There are two components to this approach to make it effective. If you miss one or both of the components in this approach, then you miss the opportunity to honor your team member. It's not about the mistake, it's about improving your organization and team.

Correct and redirect is the effort in which a leader identifies and investigates the potential error or performance concern whether it be by choice or action and then initiate the recommendation. Understanding the why and how of the error will prepare the leader to initiate the what of the correction and redirection of choice or action. Honoring others as a leader is the effort taken to ensure the team is performing properly. Should a leader identify a potential performance concern, honoring the team member is helping make the correction before it becomes too big. Some leaders may counter this approach by saying their team will become angry for being called out on a performance concern. This anger for being called out stems from having a spirit of offense. The spirit of offense is where a person immediately is angered because the team members assume they are right; their filter perceives their own performance as acceptable and even sometimes above reproach.

The spirit of offense can also speak to a team member's maturity level to be personally accountable for accepting correction and redirection. Addressing a team member with a spirit of offense can be tricky. From my experience, it is advisable to address the performance or outcome of the concern and not direct it at the person. It's the behavior of the person, not the person. If addressing anyone for a correct and redirect, do it in private.

Timely is probably the key component of the correct and redirect timely statement. If you address it quickly, then it prevents the performance concern from becoming a bigger issue or the team member creating a habit. Waiting until the annual or quarterly performance review is too late. Never let the sun go down on your anger or concern for a team member's performance concern. Address it as you identify and investigate it. So now that you have corrected and redirected, how do you initiate and handle the approach? In a previous section, we touched on team members that can claim a spirit of offense. Yes, addressing a performance concern with a team member is tough and an integral part of a leader's role.

Support and not punish is a positive approach to give a team member the right environment to make the choice to improve. When the performance concern has been addressed, providing opportunities to learn, grow and make mistakes with recognizable accountability is helpful. Punishing a team member for a mistake will create a system where the team member will avoid taking chances or thinking for opportunities to improve. Mistakes are acceptable so long as the leader communicates and supports the difference between a "misdemeanor mistake" and a "felony mistake". The team will fall on occasion and the team will make mistakes along the way. It is the leader's role to honor and help their team get back up to continue moving forward in the right direction for the organization and the team member. This does not mean that a leader will create an environment to allow for continued performance concerns, rather an environment that a team member has resources to improve, has a leader that fosters opportunities for a team member to boldly make decisions and correct and redirect along the way.

Be grateful in all things from your team. Missing this approach is where a leader will start to take the team for granted. If you have ever been taken for granted, then you recognize how it impacts you as a person. Leaders who recognize the contributions each team member makes to the overall success of an organization will fill the team with energy. Becoming grateful can be difficult for some leaders. The expectation for some leaders is again that their team gets paid to do what they do, and they should be grateful each time they get a paycheck. Well, to a point that is accurate. Hopefully, your team is grateful for a job and paycheck, but imagine how much more grateful and productive a team could be if their leader is grateful for them as a person.

Indifference comes from a lack of being grateful. This is a debilitating feeling for a leader and team to possess. With indifference, a leader will become disconnected from their team and goals. The team will also become disconnected from their job and goals. Avoid indifference and practice gratefulness by paying attention to your team and what they do and accomplish. Keeping track of what they succeed at is just as important, if not more, as identifying where they miss the mark. Here is a simple breakdown of gratefulness. Can you run your organization by yourself? If not, then be grateful you have a team. Did you drag your team off the street to work for you? If not, be grateful they chose to work with you and not your competitor. Did you have an area of success or growth in your organization? If so, then be grateful that your team contributed to it. When you are aware of your team, then you will find things to be grateful for.

Watch, listen, ask questions and be prepared to adjust your perspective to honor others.

Show appreciation is the act of recognizing the gratefulness you have for your team. You can do this for your team in a variety of ways. Whereas we correct and redirect in private, we show appreciation in public. This is the opportunity to encourage and inspire your team. Each team member has an "appreciation language" that they prefer to be appreciated through. Some simply prefer a thank you, some prefer a public display of praise and congratulations while others prefer a gift to be simply appreciated.

Missing an opportunity to show appreciation for some team members can be as harsh as a punishment. Recognize what your team needs in their "appreciation language". Examples of an "appreciation language" for your team members can include:

- Quality time with a supervisor for mentoring or feedback. The face to face time can be seen as valuable.

- Gifts can vary depending on how your team member perceives gifts. A gift can include simple items, gifts during special occasions such as holidays, work anniversaries or birthdays. Gifting can also include sharing online articles you find interesting.

- Words that encourage can fill a team member's appreciation bucket. These words can be verbal, written or electronic. It's the appreciation of meaningful words.

- Providing a service can show appreciation as well. Help on a project, a little free time for a team member to decompress can mean a lot. It does not have to be a lot, and the little support given is the appreciation.

- Physical touch can be an appreciation as well. This can be tricky but know the proper and appropriate way to appreciate your team member with a handshake, fist bump or high five can be appropriate. Be mindful of personal boundaries with this one.

Many employees will tie their worth to appreciation as much as their pay. Knowing how your team members appreciate appreciation is critical to honoring them. Spend time getting to know how they prefer appreciation. Appreciation should always be meaningful and for a reason. Avoid sharing a blanket or generalized appreciation. That approach is as empty and meaningless as not showing appreciation at all.

Wish well is certainly a necessary part of honoring others. Understandably given all the tools and efforts made to honor others, there will be moments in which a team member is not going to work. This can be one of the toughest parts of being a leader and external leadership demands that this be a part of the process.

Give honor to others to express how you perceive them as a valuable member of the team. External leadership is sharing the good things stored up within you so that others may benefit and be given opportunities to grow. Of course, I am not blind to understand that there are limits and boundaries to what a leader can and should endure to maintain the goals of the organization and team. At some point, tough decisions must be made. Should a team member choose to not perform their assigned job, then sometimes it is necessary to wish a team member well on a new journey. Given the tools provided before this point such as correct and redirect, support-not punish, be grateful and show appreciation, a leader has honored the team member so they can choose to be better and succeed. Realistically for some team members, this will never be enough no matter all the tools and chances.

Dishonoring the remaining team by not making the decision to wish a team member well can be worse than keeping the specific team member in your organization. If you do not address the team member appropriately and timely, then your other team members will become frustrated and indifferent about pushing harder for you. Don't allow a team member to dishonor your team and organization. Do not allow your lack of action to compound the dis-honor either.

Ultimately, when you get to this point given all the proper documentation necessary for employment separation, a final point of honor is simply to wish them well on their new journey. You never know, one day that team member may cross paths with you again in some capacity. There is no loss in honoring a person as they depart on a new journey, only future potential if it is meant to be.

Overall

How do you create a plan for overall leadership?

Overall leadership is the culmination of developing internal leadership for yourself and presenting a form of external leadership with your team. When these two concepts work together, you will find opportunities in which overall leadership will begin to develop and the honor you are creating begins to duplicate. So how can you duplicate honor? Duplicate leadership within your team. Let's explore some options.

Identify the leaders in your team. Every team will have one or two or more leaders that stand out, that do extra when needed and have an instinctive positive approach. These are team members that several other team members will gravitate towards. Also, look for the team members that you recognize some potential. They may not be perfect; they may make some mistakes, but they are willing to learn and improve. These are sometimes the quiet team members that observe others and are self-starters. Start with working with these team members.

Investigate growth opportunities for these identified team members. Spend time communicating and recognizing their potential. Find learning opportunities that will improve their skills. You can do this by connecting them with the right alignments in your organization, mentoring, suggesting books, podcasts or other outlets that would be beneficial. Invite them to meetings where they would normally not be invited. When you have your team members on board, then you can begin working through opportunities to grow these future leaders. As each team member is going through their growth path, stay connected, follow up and encourage.

Initiate giving away control to the leaders in your team. At this point, you have identified and investigated how to start duplicating leadership within your organization or team. When the time is right, and do not wait too long, start giving away control of decisions to the leaders within the team. Another point to share with your team during the initiate phase is explaining the differences between two types of mistakes. There are misdemeanor mistakes and felony mistakes. A misdemeanor mistake is a simple mistake, it is correctable and is not considered a showstopper. There is a relatively easy potential for recovery. Most importantly if a team lead makes a misdemeanor mistake, they do not have to fear for their job. It is a simple correct and redirect opportunity. However, the felony mistakes are more egregious and more difficult to recover. Your team leads should know and understand what this might look like in your organization or team environment. You can certainly imagine and describe examples immediately for this one. When your team understands the differences between these two types of mistakes, there is a comfort level within your team to be confident and bold in their actions. When you have confident and bold team members, then you often have a team that will go above and beyond and potentially improves efficiencies and success.

Promote your new leaders into another position or elevate their awareness with the other team members. Giving additional responsibilities to your team is a function of honor stemming from trust and confidence in their potential abilities. When you identify the team members, investigate how you will boost their ongoing opportunities and initiate the control to do more, find ways to promote their new success. Announce to other team members and the organization that this team member has been elevated into their role. If there is an opportunity, promote from within for the vacant position. This is a sure sign that you have trust in your current team and their growth. However, you can promote your new team leads to elevate their awareness of your trust in them, they will then begin to look to elevate others at the same time. This is where you will continue to see honor and leadership growth within your team and organization. When you build your team up through positive leadership including a process of internal leadership, external leadership and overall leadership you begin to deposit confidence, positivity, awareness, appreciation and gratitude in the structure of your organization and team.

To drive the point home further, Bruce J. Avolio and William Gardner in their research article announced that in the initial framework of authentic leadership (read positive leadership) there must be positive psychological capital. Or said in another way, internal positivity includes confidence, optimism, hope and resiliency. Positive psychological capital or internal positivity is what you possess within you. What you hold internalized. In order to purchase something, you need capital. In order to perform as a positive leader, you need positive psychological capital or internal positivity.

To create psychological capital or internal positivity, there is a standard method in which most will look to build capital and that example is through the banking system. Let's explore how leaders can build this capital following a proven approach.

Bank On It

There is an opportunity to investigate a way to build layers of positive capital with your team through maintaining a Positive Leadership Bank Account. This is how you create your process to start investing in yourself and your team as a positive leader. Here is where you can manage the exchange of honor for, from, to and within your team. Understanding this allows you to bank on creating a way in which to understand or recognize actions taken are similar to how a banking system works. When a team knows a leader is banking on them, there is a buildup of confidence.

Transactional banking is where the customer and the banking teller exchange a one and done service. You will find a lot of leaders are quick to fall into a transactional banking approach with their team. Here is the assignment, get the work done, go home and return the next day to do it again. Nothing more, nothing less. To Bank On It as a positive leader with your team, transformational banking is the best approach. We will explore more in-depth transformational versus transaction later in this book. Understand in this sense, a transformational banker will create a relationship with their customer. A positive leader using a transformational banking approach will create a positive relationship with their team.   Let's look at some terminology from the banking system and how you can apply it to positive leadership to create a transformational banking mindset with your team.

Deposits are the appreciation you share with your team as a leader. Appreciation is your currency exchanged with your team that creates the deposit in their accounts. As with any bank having a positive balance is ideal. In order to maintain a positive balance with your team as a positive leader, you will need to make deposits greater than your withdrawals. If your appreciation currency is real and not counterfeit, you can make your teams wealthy.

Withdrawals are missed opportunities to support your team. Here you will find withdrawals happening when support turns to punishment. There is correct but no redirect. Or a wish well for a team member is not done or done timely. When you get into withdrawals there are chances of incurring fees. Fees can come in the form of grumblings, rumors and outright griping. Withdrawals have a greater impact on your team than deposits. It is critical to recognize when a withdrawal occurs and even more important to know your account balance after a withdrawal. Withdrawals should be followed quickly with the right deposits into the organization or team's positive psychological capital.

Interest is the additional appreciation currency obtained from maintaining a positive balance. When your team has a sufficient balance, you will begin to find that interest starts accruing. Interest in you as a leader, interest in your team's potential and success. You will begin to see the interest start compounding as well as your team will be able to make positive deposits into other team members' accounts.

Loans are banking terms in which you borrow something with an intent to give it back. One way I would honor my team is to honor their most precious resource: time. I have hosted meetings on a regular basis, so it is my responsibility to be prepared and stay on time. Of course, invariably we will go over our allotted meeting time due to the length of the agenda topics or questions and conversations stemming from the agenda topics. I would make a point to recognize the time remaining or the time we went over. If we went over, that was time in my team's bank that I took a loan out. It was my responsibility to recognize it, identify it with the team and then pay it back at the next meeting. If we went over our meeting time during the previous meeting, then I would do everything possible to give their time back from the following meeting. Understandably, this is a minor item: borrowing my team's time for a needed meeting.

Loans can also be in the form of pushing an organization or team hard to meet a goal. Or to react to something that is urgent and may require overtime or beyond normal effort to make happen. Pressing on a team periodically is expected as business is uncertain. However, loans are loans and it is important to recognize and pay back the time and effort from the organization and team with a reward, a treat or something that would fill their appreciation bucket. Here is the issue, if leaders do not honor the little things regarding their team, then how will they trust their leader or each other in the big things?

Return on Investment or ROI is another banking term in which a person will give something of value to another person with the understanding and trust that the other person will do something of value with it to make that something of value grow. The two key terms here are value and trust. What are the things of value that one person can give another? What most people will think of first is money. As a leader, your team gives you their time, attention and future leadership opportunities to you. Recognizing that the leadership and the edification you provide your team is a double investment. This investment not only allows for team members to grow in their knowledge, skills and talents, it also improves their efficiency, productivity and future leadership potential. Your investment has a potential double ROI.

The only way in which a team member will allow you to invest in their resource of time, attention and future leadership opportunities is through trust. To get to a potential double ROI on investment is through trust. The honor you give yourself and your team will inherently build that trust for future investments resulting in multiplying your return on investment.

Ready for some insider trading secrets and knowledge on potential positive leadership budgeting tips to be mindful of as well? Don't write leadership checks you have no intention of backing or leadership promises your team cannot cash. This is where a lot of leaders will end up creating more withdrawals for their team due to unfulfilled promises. At this point, the environment is in Appreciation Debt. This scenario is a critical stage to recognize and is important to recover as quickly as possible.

Appreciation Debt Recovery

If you ever walk into an environment or have inadvertently created an environment or circumstance where positive leadership and the positive bank accounts of your team are over withdrawn or are on the verge of bankruptcy, then you know this can become a panic-ridden stock market crash feeling. There are tools in which you can address the current negative balances and build positive leadership gains. Appreciation Debt is a path to moral bankruptcy. It can devastate your team and organization. Recovery is a required approach. A leader should immediately investigate how to get your organization and team's balances back into the positive.

An **Emergency Fund** is how you start something simple to support a positive environment. Identify where you can begin an ongoing function within the organization or team to recognize positive outcomes from your team, no matter how small. This should be an ongoing event or process. Even if it is as simple as hosting a weekly meeting and discussing successes from the week before. Or creating a challenge to meet certain reasonable, quick, win-type goals that your team can accomplish and start to feel good about themselves. Here you are simply looking to start making deposits and building up a positive balance so that the organization and team sees, understands and feels you are looking to support and not punish at every turn.

Momentum is where you will identify the areas and levels of appreciation debt within your team and organization. At this point, you will need to strategize how you will address the levels of appreciation debt in the different areas. Continue to bank positive capital with your team and look for ways to deposit extra positive appreciation into the accounts of your team members that are not too overdrawn. Fill up the accounts of those that are the least overdrawn first. Start building momentum with the emergency fund appreciation deposits. When you can get a few team members into a positive balance, then you can engage their support to continue to build the appreciation and positivity momentum with the remaining team members until you have a positive balance across the board.

Invest in your team members once you have established your Emergency Fund of appreciation and have brought your team or organization through the momentum process. An investment in your team is recognizing work anniversaries, birthdays or other milestones in their career or personal life. Here you can create a game plan to host annual award ceremonies to recognize outstanding performances. Make a point to recognize a team member or department of the month. These are consistently professional and personal deposits into your team and organization's appreciation bank account.

Generosity will come in a few forms. You can give appreciation to your team individually, through awards and public recognition. These are highly effective. When you have recovered from appreciation debt and filled the positive bank accounts of your team, the biggest form of deposits will come through generosity. Not simply generosity from the leader, but from peer to peer. When your team has a filled appreciation positive bank account, they will be able to become generous with each other. You will find them giving praise and appreciation all around. Not to downgrade the importance of a leader's appreciation, but a peer to peer form of generosity will typically mean the most to fellow team members.

Identifying how you plan to Bank On It and address Appreciation Debt Recovery gives you the guidance to initiate building your team positive psychological capital. You now have several steps and plans to keep the balances positive and create a wealthy organization and team. Bank On It provides the how to keep the balances full. Appreciation Debt Recovery is your how to simply put into practice external leadership through honoring others and then eventually reaping overall leadership by duplicating honor within your team. It takes a process to get through these steps. The level of wealth in positive psychological capital, your organization and team development, ultimately stems from you as the leader developing internal leadership and creating a positive leadership mindset. Your mindset will constantly be under pressure. Our human instinct to be negative along with the external hurdles and obstacles faced through leadership can be overwhelming at times.

Battle Ground

Overcoming internal negativity and external obstacles and hurdles includes filling your own positive bank accounts and most importantly battling for the right mindset. This is an everyday process for some leaders. Others may struggle with it periodically when the going gets tough. The only way to get to the point of becoming a banker of positive psychological capital is to battle your mindset. What does it look like to recognize the difference between a negative and positive leadership mindset to get you there? What kind of battle will you face and what are the weapons between the two? Let's explore the two different leadership mindset approaches and how they will impact your level of success and your team or organization's level of success. This is a full-on battle that wages on!

Negative Leadership Mindset	Positive Leadership Mindset
Have to	Want to
Taker	Giver
Reactive	Proactive
Effect	Affect
Me	Us
Wing It	Experience
Little Picture	Big Picture

How you investigate the differences between the negative and positive leadership mindset will prepare you with a new filter and perception.   Or better said, the weapon to overcome the enemy of the mind is by giving you more powerful weapons and fighting strategies for a positive leadership mindset. This recognizable perception of thinking, speaking and acting will determine your success as well.   This is a battle of two mindsets. To be honest with you, there can only be one mindset at a time.   You fight to win or you will lose by default.   There must be a clear and decisive winner, no judge's decision, it must be a TKO in the first round.   The winner will be the one you give attention to, the one that you feed and the one you literally fight for on a regular basis.   In my first book The SUPERFANTASTIC Principles, we explore how humans have a negative bias, an instinctual protection mode towards the negative. So, this will be an ongoing battle.   However, through your intentional thoughts, your intentional speech and your intentional actions you can overcome to create a new and stronger battle-ready positive mindset, a positive leadership mindset.

Let's look at our leadership fight card.   In the ring or at least within your mind, you will find the champion and challenger.   It is an underdog versus instinctual crowd favorite. Who are you betting on?   What are the odds between the two as they battle it out in your mind?

Let's get ready to RUUUUUUUUUMBLE!

Have to versus Want to* is a nasty battle. This is where your perception of how you do things start. If you wake up in the morning and the first thing you say is, I have to get up, I have to get ready for work, I have to do all this work, then you are already done for the day. Some of you may remember an old Dunkin Donuts commercial of the guy waking early in the morning stating "time to make the donuts" with a defeated look and attitude, that is a have to mindset. No one likes to have to do anything. It is a self-defeating perception. So, what is the alternative to Have to? Want to. Battle for this mindset each day.

An I want to mindset, sets you up with a positive approach to do battle. This is the "faith it until you make it" motto. Say it before you do anything. It is an intentional choice and action, even if it is a thought in your mind, say I want to [*fill in the blank*]. This is where you prepare your mind to drudge through something or positively attack the thing. Say it again with me: I want to [*fill in the blank with your next assignment*]. This is how you start making the shift, cleaning your window of perception and sharpening your fighting skills. This is your jabbing in the battle, simple yet effective overtime.

*Let me add a side note regarding another positive mindset fighter. Get to and Want to are very similar positive mindset fighters. You can interchange the two fighters in this battle within reason. The reason I chose Want to in this example is because in my perception, Get to creates a perception that the opportunity is there to do something. But for me, it falls just short of actually doing it. Whereas Want to creates a perception that the opportunity is there and I am actively about to make it happen. For me, Get to is the emotion and Want to is the E-Motion. Remember, go with the verb!

Taker versus Giver is a battle of tearing down or building up. The taker's mindset is about being distrustful of others and not likely to offer help. Distrust of others, especially in your organization or team, destroys confidence. When a leader is not able to trust an organization or team, you are tearing down any confidence and willingness from your organization and team to do what they should do, much less go above and beyond. The team gets stuck in their ruts and routines because as a leader with a taker mindset, you only want to take the work your team does and nothing else. This mindset of only taking from your team is a tough pounding given to your team over time. The morale will not last long in this fight. Whereas a giver mindset is devoting yourself to develop others who show motivation to grow.

When a leader identifies a team member that is eager, willing to learn and goes above and beyond, the giver mindset can kick into gear creating further motivation and opportunity for this team member. Another benefit of the giver mindset is that other team members will recognize it and join the fight adopting the giver mindset as well. Sooner than you think, you will have a team and organization of giver fighters supporting each other. This is a one-sided fight when the giver mindset takes over. There is nothing that a taker mindset can do to overcome when giver mindsets are in control. Givers will get takers against the ropes and the fight will not last much longer before the ref calls it.

Reactive versus Proactive is the classic battle of defense against offense. In football, you hear defense wins championships. However, in a positive leadership mindset match, the offense of having a proactive mindset will win the overall leadership battle. With a reactive mindset, you wait for problems to occur. In some instances, a reactive mindset will see the problem, know that it is coming, recognizes the issues it will create and yet still waits for it to punch the leader, team and organization in the gut before taking action. Or the reactive leadership mindset is constantly hiding behind their gloves, in anticipation of something happening, and not able to see what is going on because their vision of what is around them is blocked.

Nothing is ever ventured behind the reactive leadership mindset. When you embrace the proactive mindset, you have a clear vision of what is going on. You can see the problems coming and can attack them before the problems get too overwhelming. Of course, with a proactive mindset, you will take some hits, but that is part of the battle. Even the reactive mindset will take hits. The big difference is with a proactive mindset you can see the punches coming and have a chance to fix it, move it or even use it to your advantage. There will be pain in both fights, so pick the pain you want to endure. When you face the oncoming issues before they become a problem, the proactive mindset will win the fight.

Effect versus Affect can be a confusing brawl. It is that one letter difference between the two words that is the fancy footwork in your match. Think about it this way – effect mindset is barely fighting; in fact, it is simply taking the hits as they come because you become the result of the punches. An affect mindset is taking the fight to the circumstance because you are making the changes around you. When a negative mindset fights, it uses effect and the result of how things happen. It's a very similar fighting style to the reactive mindset. Your effect mindset will just take a "how things are" fight to that circumstance. It is the "this is how we have always done it" approach to fighting. They become the result of the environment. Whereas when fighting using an affect mindset, you create the environment, you take the fight to the situation. The thoughts, speech and actions you have make things happen how you want them. You are not defined by the world around you because you are creating the world around you. You see the world, environment or circumstance in its current state and define how it will be after you are part of it. The affect mindset will dominate the fight by keeping the effect mindset on its heels.

Me versus Us mindset is a selfish game against a fulfilling game. A me mindset simply wants to fight for one thing or one person, usually themselves. But in this approach, when the going gets tough, and it will, there is no backup. No one is around to support this fighter when they need help. Others can spot a me mindset quickly and will try to avoid that fighter at all cost. Using the us mindset in a fight creates an army of people that will battle together to support each other. Here you will find some people will take the hits to protect another team member. Some will jump out in front to alert others to oncoming issues. The greatest part of the us mindset is that there will always be someone in your corner when you need to tag in another fighter or get the sweat wiped from your brow. There is power in this numbers game. The us mindset will almost always overpower the feeble and selfish me mindset.

Wing It versus Experience plays the novice against the professional. This should be an easy pick for your battle, but all too often I have seen leaders select the wrong mindset here. A wing it mindset is trying to figure out the fight as you are in the battle similar to the reactive mindset. There are a lot of wild punches and swinging with this mindset. It is fast and furious with your eyes closed flailing about. Rarely will this mindset have an effective fight. On the experience side, it is a little slower, more methodical and much more intentional. To be honest the experience mindset can be frustrating for some as it does not move as fast as others. Some even try to combine the wing it and experience fighters to move things forward only to find that they will eventually turn on each other. Experience mindset uses the past successes and failures as a framework on how to make decisions. Even a new leader will have experiences to draw from when creating a fighting plan. It may not be from their own experience but from the experiences of other leaders in their career path. It is a calculated thought before a punch is thrown. A wing it mindset will usually get knocked out by itself in the first round and the experience mindset will go the distance.

Little Picture versus Big Picture is your final battleground of mindsets. Your mindset choice has a lot to do with your level of success. You can choose from a variety of mindsets or have your opponent choose it for you. Selecting your mindsets such as Want To, Giver, Proactive, Affect, Us and Experience is a winning combination in any battle. The alternative, not so much. When you align your mindset correctly, like having the right alignments in your life, you can get through almost any obstacle or battle that comes your way. Our positive mindsets allow us to work with us in a positive manner, it is a function of internal leadership that allows for a successful implementation of external leadership. The little picture versus the big picture is the battle for everything. This is the war for overall leadership.

A negative mindset using little picture thinking or fighting technique will focus on the here and now. They will do little to stand up and walk out of their own corner to get in the fight. What works now. This is how we have always done it. What is the minimum I need to do in order to get through this very moment? How can I work the least without having to do anymore? It is me, my work, my project for today and nothing else. Sound familiar? We have all been there. When morale is low and motivation is lacking, we become head down and oblivious to anything else beyond the immediate moment. There is little fight in this approach.

Growing into the big picture mindset of a positive leader takes all the other positive leadership mindsets combined to become this unstoppable fighter. How does what I decide now impact today, tomorrow and beyond? Recognizing that every decision made in the moment creates a ripple that will connect with outcomes tomorrow. This becomes a thoughtful mindset of viewing the environment and circumstances differently. I have seen leaders in my experience use this approach many times. It changes the game plan, it changes the way you identify, investigate and initiate your moves. This punch may take time to land on the opponent, but when it does the fight is over. It is the ultimate TKO knockout.

Prepare yourself for fierce battles between the negative and positive mindsets. Know I am in your corner, coaching you through the fight, giving you guidance as you catch your breath between rounds and strategizing for the knock-out punch. The negative mindsets have inherent weaknesses and it is our responsibility to identify them, investigate how to get around them and initiate the decisive blow to become victorious over them. It comes down to choice and action for each fight. It comes down to choice and action for every approach, every process you will take. Becoming a positive leader will not guarantee success in every situation. It will though give you courage and confidence to go up against the toughest battles. Positive leadership will give you the mindset, perception and filter that you can do more than you ever thought possible. And identifying and investigating what you can do is a big win in my book.

We are getting you geared up to start initiating all that we have discussed, reviewed and learned in the previous sections. There is a process to make the can do become an action. You are a winner. You are on your way to becoming a positive leader and will make incredibly positive things happen for yourself and others, if you choose to do so and take action.

Investigate: Positive Leadership *Wrapped Up*

Internal Leadership	Honor Yourself by connecting yourself with the right alignments and mentors. Fill your atmosphere by reading, watching and learning positive information that will benefit your growth.
External Leadership	Honor Others by correcting and redirecting timely, supporting and not punishing, being grateful, showing appreciation and wishing well when necessary.
Overall Leadership	Duplicate Honor by identifying new leaders, investigating opportunities, initiating control to the new leaders and promoting these opportunities with the team.
Bank On it	Layering positive capital into your team's morale bank accounts. Being mindful of your transactions.
Appreciation Debt Recovery	The plan to climb out of a negative balance of morale bank accounts through appropriate budgeting tools.
Battle Ground	The battle fought over your mindset. There are two mindsets fighting over your attention, negative and positive. The mindset that you give your attention and intention will normally win.

ACTION & STEPS: Process Planning Notes

Question	Your Thoughts
Identify why you perceive/filter "Positive Leadership" the way you do.	
Investigate how you would elevate your "Positive Leadership"?	
Initiate what would be your "Positive Leadership"?	
Additional Considerations	

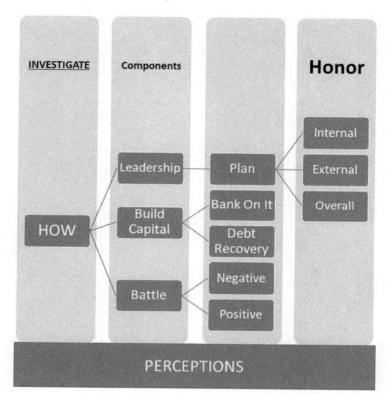

Chapter 2   Investigate: POSITIVE LEADERSHIP

Check Yourself Chapter

Prepare to Initiate: THINK, SPEAK, ACT

"Examine yourselves, to see whether you are in the faith. Test yourselves."
2 Corinthians 13:5

The rubber is about to meet the road. We have identified the overall components of Positivity and Leadership along with numerous concepts to get us prepared for this part of the book. We have investigated the positive leadership components as well. This is where we take the knowledge and apply it. Take action, or better said, initiate. Intentions mean nothing if not applied. Marie Forleo is quoted as saying, "Show up every single moment like you're meant to be there." Because you are. You have been given an opportunity to make a positive difference with each opportunity only if you initiate it.

Another ubiquitous statement seen and heard is "just do it". I agree with this statement in part. I believe you should prepare before you just do it. I know that goes against the intention of the actual quote but hear me out. When you just do it, you end up doing it based on what you have filled your mind, spoken and acted upon or worse yet, what you are feeling at the moment. Your just do it is done with the filters or perceptions you have created. As we identified earlier depending on your approach, negative or positive, your just do it can be very different. Before you travel down this road to prepare on becoming a Positive Think, Speak, Act Leader, I want you to check yourself. What do I mean by check yourself? Let's discuss a few points to consider. Get ready to put into action the new filter you will be using.

WHAT IT IS...

Here is what you can control. The world around you is not in your control. The people around you are not in your

55

control. The only thing you have ultimate control over are these three things: your thoughts, your speech and your actions. This is the sphere in which you have ultimate control. View it this way, draw a circle around yourself and everything inside is what you can control. If you attempt to control others outside your sphere or circle, you are overreaching your sphere and will fall on your face most of the time. That is all. So, let's start to prepare what's in our own circle.

When you prepare, when you take intentional steps to just do it, then your just do it has a greater potential for success. I truly believe that the process of intentionally preparing your think, speak and act will get you to a better position. What is needed to prepare?

The following are some tough statements to absorb. Until you truly understand, accept and prepare your perception of what I share next, the following chapters will be useless to you.

You are thinking what you are thinking because you have allowed it. You can decide what you will think next.

You are speaking the way you speak because you have allowed it. You can decide what you will say next.

You are acting the way you are acting because you have allowed it. You can decide the way you want to act next.

You are why, who and what you have allowed yourself to be.

Many will blame their circumstance, their environment, their family or friends for the why, who and what they are. This is a convenient excuse because it deflects the blame. It gives a person comfort to not be responsible for why, who, what and where they are. A default mindset will look to find blame outside than to find accountability inside.

You can decide to use the experiences as a tool to grow. Or you can use your experiences as an excuse to continue to blame other people or things. A design mindset will find accountability inside and search for opportunities for responsibility on the outside. Right here and right now, you have two options. Defer personal responsibility for your future to other people, places or things. Or your second option, which I highly recommend, is to take personal accountability for your future based on your Think, Speak and Act. That's it. Those are the two options you must work with. Committing to be accountable for your sphere is an action step to take the next step. It is you, no one else will be able to do it for you. No one else can make you change except you and it all stems from being accountable that you are in control of what you allow you to think, speak and act.

I'll even go deeper with this conversation. This is the real SHIFT. And I promise you, SHIFT happens, when you choose to change. Imagine, if you will, an example of a person accidentally choosing to SHIFT in their life. Let's call our example person Sam and see how a momentary SHIFT from Sam makes a significant change.

Day one – Sam drives to work listening to the same talk radio show in his car and dives headfirst into his work, takes lunch, continues with his work and then drives home at the end of the day.

Day two - Sam drives to work listening to the same talk radio show in his car and dives headfirst into his work, takes lunch, continues with his work and then drives home at the end of the day.

Day three turns to year five - Sam drives to work listening to the same talk radio show in his car and dives headfirst into his work, takes lunch, continues with his work and then drives home at the end of the day.

Year five and one day – Sam drives to work listening to the same talk radio show in his car and just before he dives headfirst into his work he randomly and out of routine looks up and sees an opportunity. Sam thinks to himself, how long has this opportunity been available? Curiosity overcomes Sam enough to speak to his supervisor about the opportunity. Sam asks his supervisor, how long has this opportunity been available? Sam's supervisor responds to Sam that the opportunity has been available since Sam started.

Sam at this time is shocked and dismayed by what he just heard. Sam knows that this opportunity would be perfect for him. It would make a huge positive difference in his life. In Sam's mind a thousand questions were swirling around: Why had he not heard about it until now? Why didn't his supervisor bring it to his attention? Why is he just now seeing this opportunity? How many other opportunities did I miss? Do you see how the blaming starts so quickly? How easy it is to think it is someone else's responsibility to do for you?

Sam gathers his composure stands up straight and looks at his supervisor with a bit of defeat in his posture and asks, "Why didn't you ever tell me about this opportunity before?" Sam's supervisor pauses, looks at the opportunity and then back at Sam and says, "You never asked."

Now, let's overlook the fact that Sam's supervisor should have done a better job at supporting Sam in his career (and will probably do so after reading this book) and focus on Sam's responsibility to his own career. Did Sam do anything wrong? You could say yes and no. He faithfully went to work. He diligently did his work. But what Sam missed was his SHIFT.

Sam did what he did year after year but missed looking up and around. He missed looking for opportunities to improve his life. He thought and relied on other people to bring opportunities to his attention. Sam was in a default mode for all these years. Sam allowed his thoughts, his speech and actions to be determined by a default routine. Imagine all the other opportunities Sam may have missed while living a default life in a default routine. When you make a SHIFT in your choice and action, you start to begin to look up and out of your default mindset. You take control of a default routine and break free of its grip on you. You SHIFT from default to design, from negative to positive. This SHIFT is the breakthrough. Instead of walking this way, walk the other way.

Now replace Sam's name with your own name. Now replace the word opportunity in the story with the "something" that you could do or become. When and where will your SHIFT occur? Your SHIFT will allow you to understand that you can decide to make a change. Don't be Sam, be SHIFTy.

You can decide and initiate what you will THINK, what you will SPEAK and what you will ACT. What does it mean to initiate? Up until now, we have identified why positivity and leadership are valuable and important. We have also investigated how you can create a plan or strategy to become a positive leader. Now we need to act. We need to make things happen. At this point, we are ready to prepare to just do it because we have an internalized guide that supports it. Initiate is when you put the key in the ignition and turn on the car to go where you want to go. You cannot make a shift if you are standing still. You cannot move to the next level blindly either. Even before putting the key in the ignition, you need to make sure you complete several steps in the process. Learning to drive, practice driving, taking a test, getting your license, making sure your car has gas, tires inflated, seatbelt on, seat adjusted, mirrors positioned, (proper driving music on) and so much more. These are all critical steps to prepare before you drive off, before you just do it.

Just as you do all the things before driving a car, one must prepare equally before driving off on your THINK, SPEAK and ACT. Let's start by checking yourself before we get into the initiation. You have the why and the how, let's talk about you. Here is the first check I want you to determine.

Are you committed to making a change?

This in of itself is a challenging question. Since you have made it this far in the book, then I am confident you are leaning toward making the SHIFT and committed to the change of becoming a positive THINK, SPEAK, ACT leader or you are looking to elevate where you are now. Either way, this is the toughest part to hold on to. Unless you are committed to make the change and stay with it, then you will eventually fall back into the default side of life. You will fall back into the Sam or SHIFT-less routine with your head down missing the opportunities.

Let's explore some ways to pull back the curtain on yourself and identify and investigate who and how you are before you initiate the SHIFT.

Connections and Tools

How can you know yourself to check yourself? What types of connections and tools are available to support you in and through this process? There are an incredible amount of connections and tools to give you an opportunity to create a relatively objective look at yourself. I will share a short list of options, and by no means is this an exhaustive list to check yourself. Let me warn you though, even the best of tools is flawed. These are meant to give you a starting point or reference point to begin to make changes. Diving deep into check yourself mode can lead down a lot of different rabbit holes that can be tough to climb out. Use the feedback, the information you receive from the connections and tools below as a place to start, to recognize your filters and perspectives.

If you cannot recognize or become aware of your perspective or filter, then you lose the opportunity to make the SHIFT. Below are some connections and tools to begin checking yourself.

Alignments should be your first source for feedback. An alignment is a person or people you trust to give you honest feedback. They will not sugar coat feedback to prevent you from being offended and they will also temper their feedback in a way that is constructive, not destructive. Prepare questions before challenging your alignment(s) to give you feedback. If possible, prepare your alignment by providing some questions and giving them time to think through it and prepare for feedback. Ask for detailed examples if possible. When it comes to feedback, generalities are not terribly useful.

Mentors will help coach you through your current state. Know what your goals and vision are before meeting with a mentor. Use the time with a mentor to fine tune your thoughts, plans and goals. Mentors will typically have a lot of experience from a variety of perspectives and can give you guidance and feedback on the plans you have made. They may not tell you how to do it or what to do, but they will push you to think through your goal and vision in a unique and inspiring way. A mentor will also encourage and inspire you to press forward after talking through everything.

DISC And Myers Briggs are a behavioral assessment tool used to identify personality types. DISC breaks up personalities into four parts identifying at what levels you respond to issues, influence others, respond to rules and procedures and prefer the pace of activity. Myers Briggs sorts personalities into 16 different types. Both options have value and provide valuable insight into how you are. One explores your internal thinking and the other explores your external behavior. You can find several options to take the assessments to identify how you are. The purpose of this assessment is to use it as a tool to improve your work productivity, teamwork, leadership and communication. Unless you know you, it is difficult to change you. A quick search online will find you several different personality assessments and information.

Personal Inventories give you a chance to review yourself in a personal way. This is a means to document what you feel to be important and meaningful aspects of your life. This could include strengths, weaknesses, successes, failures, missed opportunities and so much more. Here it is important to use a SMART goal approach with your planning of your SHIFT. Specific, Measurable, Accountable, Relatable and Timely. If you are not able to press in and be honest with the self-reflection of yourself, then you will be less likely to be honest with others. These are the things that define you as a person.

There is a lot of work to prepare to check yourself. This is a tough part of the process to go through, especially when you start feeling exposed. The final question you will need to answer for yourself and before we get into the initiate your THINK, SPEAK and ACT is:

Do you "want to" connect your choices to your actions?

This is not a "get to" and definitely not a "have to" scenario. It is simply a question you ask yourself, "Do I want to do this?" If you say no, my next question is, "How is it working out for you now?" If there is room for improvement, then it would be advisable to reassess your perspective. You don't have to do anything; you get to do a lot of things, but you do not necessarily have to do those things. When you want to do something, there is nothing that will stop you. When you connect your choices to your actions, you become intentional. There is a SHIFT in your opportunities when you connect choice and action. In order to become intentional and create a SHIFT in your opportunities, it takes a process to check yourself. One last time I will ask, "Do you want to connect your choices to your actions?"

WARNING: Ghost Ahead!

Checking yourself can feel like you are exposing yourself to you and the world. It is not always comfortable. There is one thing that I want to bring to your attention while going through this part of the process, a **spirit of offense**. Spirit of offense is probably the most powerful deterrent in checking yourself. The spirit of offense is not a friendly spirit like Casper. It is one of those ugly, jealous and spiteful spirits that can cause a lot of damage to you and others if you let it get out of control. You can control it. You have ultimate power over a spirit of offense.

If you feel yourself getting angry or hurt while checking yourself, take a moment and reflect why you are getting mad, why the feedback is getting to you and why you are letting it get to you. If you are connecting with the right alignments and mentors, then what is shared with you may be exposing, but it is not meant to be hurtful. It is the perspective in which you view the feedback that will make the difference. One perspective is through the spirit of offense and the other is through the perspective of checking yourself to get better. Even a tool used may come back with feedback that can give you moments to pause and think about why and how you do things. Again, your perspective will determine how you use the information and feedback.

Being mindful of the spirit of offense will allow you to become more productive through the check yourself process. This process is not easy, and it never ends. It is an ongoing process. With all the things to consider including identifying your why, investigating the how of your plan and then finally initiating the plan, what is the time and practical cost of all of this? If you are business-minded or a practical thinker, then you are considering what is my ROI (return on investment) with all this work and preparing to become a Positive Think, Speak and Act Leader? My question back to you is - *What is the alternative?* If you are stuck in a default comfortable routine another question is - *How is that working out for you now?*

Get yourself unstuck! Recognize what you are holding onto from the past. The past is heavy and does not move easily. What is it that is keeping you where you are now? Check it, exercise your spirit of offense, then unstick it. When you let go of the past and reach for the future, you become free to build a better you.

If you have spent time checking yourself, you are ready. If you are ready, then let's go. Let's initiate the plan! Get ready to THINK, SPEAK and ACT your way to becoming a POSITIVE LEADER!

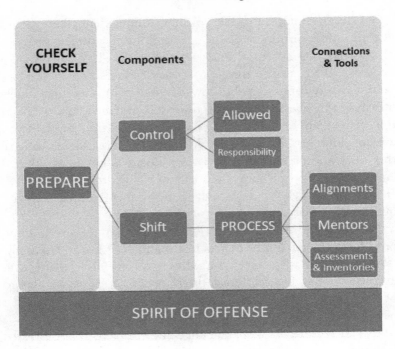

Chapter 3

Initiate: THINK

"Finally, brothers and sisters, whatever is true, whatever is noble, whatever is right, whatever is pure, whatever is lovely, whatever is admirable – if anything is excellent or praiseworthy – think about such things." Philippians 4:8

Before we begin, let me be the first to help fill your heart with something positive. Read this and let it fill your mind.

I am SUPERFANTASTIC!

Now, do not dismiss this statement. You may be grumbling about self-talk or the perceived daily self-affirmation. Work with me here. Remember, you agreed earlier in the book to say yes to your potential or you would not have made it this far in the book. Ok, I want you to read this statement again. In fact, I want you to participate in a little experiment with me. Re-read this statement in your mind at least seven times. And with conviction. If you do not read it with conviction and believe it, then you will find it difficult to encourage yourself in any other manner. Let it soak in your mind, let it be internalized to a point that you believe it. Okay, now that you have participated in this little experiment, we can move on.
We will come back to this later.

How would you feel if I shared with you that this is the start or stopping place of all your potential success? Of course, I recognize success can be defined differently for each person, so for this question, let's presuppose that success will be defined as a positive outcome of some nature, reaching a positive ongoing result or a positive ongoing opportunity. Again, let's presuppose that any struggles, obstacles, barriers will be defined as opportunities. What approach would you take with your thinking?

Let me ask the question again, how would you feel if getting your mind positive will light the path to your success? It allows you to be better than you were the day before. It allows you to prepare better today than you were yesterday. It creates opportunities to improve your personal and professional life. The approach you select will create intentionality either by default or design. Your approach is where your potential success is held. All your thoughts will therefore be by default or by design. There is no other way. Either approach you select is what you allow. What you allow is how you think. A default thinking approach allows you to be an effect of your environment. A design thinking approach allows you to critically think about your environment. Before we get into this, let's talk about science because, for me, knowing the source of my thoughts helps me appreciate the why of how I am thinking.

BRAIN SCIENCE!

Let's look at a little science of the mind and our thoughts. It's hard to believe and comprehend that the three pounds of grey matter contained between our ears stored in a hard casing is what stores so much information and drives our perception of how we interact with the world around us. Some interesting facts about the brain according to Northwestern Medicine include:

- 60% of the brain is composed of fat. – *They do say the brain is a muscle and should be exercised.*
- Your brain's storage capacity is virtually unlimited. – *I have certainly experienced moments in which I felt my brain was full after a tough day.*
- Brain information travels up to 268 miles per hour. – *No wonder they say your mind is always racing.*
- It's a myth that we only use 10% of our brain. – *Oh, how I work too hard to use it all…*
- A piece of brain tissue, the size of a grain of sand, contains 100,000 neurons and 1 billion synapses.

- The human brain can generate about 23 watts of power (enough to power a lightbulb). *This gives a new meaning to the cartoon light bulb above your head when you have an idea.*

With all the interesting facts (well, the nerdy part of me thinks they are interesting) about the brain, what is it that creates the perception of thought?   Scientists are hard-pressed to identify the true origin of thought due to the extreme complexity of the brain. Rather the focus of a thought is easier to map from the external stimuli.

Elizabeth Dougherty from MIT School of Engineering shares about tracing the origin of a thought in the brain, "Simpler, then to start by considering perceptions— 'thoughts' that are directly triggered by external stimuli—a feather brushes your skin, you see words on a computer screen, you hear a phone ring. Each of these events triggers a series of signals in the brain."

External stimuli are important. But what about internal stimuli? Internal stimuli are the stimuli that come from within the body. For example, when your body needs food because it is low on energy, it creates an internal stimulus to encourage you to eat.

At the risk of getting too deep, I want to scratch the surface of this subject a little more. What are the internal stimuli that generate our thoughts, our creativity, our feelings and emotions? For most, people will describe that their internal stimuli will come from the environment, circumstances around them. You will hear people say, I was inspired by the sunset to paint this masterpiece.   I was saddened by the event that occurred and from that circumstance, I reacted a certain way. Or that made me feel this way, so I did something. In my view, this is reactive internal stimuli.

This is potentially true if you live on the default side of life. When you are stuck in the default mode, you can only react to the things that happen around you. You become an effect of life.   However, let's keep digging into a design approach to internal stimuli. Understanding that you can become proactive to events, environments and circumstances around you allows you to affect the world around you. For example, if something is occurring around you, you decide to do something to affect the outcome of the event or circumstance. This is a foundational approach of creating a mindset of being positive and proactive in your think. It is truly important to discover what the foundation of the think, speak, act process. So, let's build on the think, the foundation. What are thoughts, what does it mean to think? Science Daily expands on the discussion of thoughts:

Thought or thinking is a mental process that allows beings to model the world, and so to deal with it effectively according to their goals, plans, ends and desires.

I find this interesting that our thoughts create a perception of the world for us to interact with it. Not only interact with it, but to do something to it or with it based on what we want. What we do to it or with it (goals, plans, ends and desires) stems from our why. This is our purpose within the world. Without a purpose, you will continually be an effect of the world as opposed to affecting the world.

Thinking involves manipulation of information, as when we form concepts, engage in problem-solving, reason and making decisions.

From our why we develop the how. How will we be able to manipulate the world around us so that we can accomplish our goals, plans, ends and desires? To get to the how, all the information we have flows through our filter or perceptions. Perceptions are how we manipulate information to form our concepts, problem solving, reason and decisions. The decisions we make fit the perception of how a problem should be solved through our perception of the problem.

The basic mechanics of the human brain reflect a process of pattern matching or rather a recognition.

In a "moment of reflection," new situations and new experiences are judged against recalled ones and judgments are made.

In order to make these judgments, the intellect maintains present experience and sorts relevant past experience.

To speak on our thoughts and ultimately act on our thoughts, we must match against our previous patterns or experiences. What is our perception of the previous patterns and experiences? If our perception of these previous patterns and experiences are negative, then our judgment will follow accordingly. If our perception is positive, then that becomes our judgment. It becomes a matching game as determined by our perception. But where do those perceptions come from? These patterns or recalled experiences come from what we allow in our minds. What we allow to be our focus, to grab our attention.

YOUR ATTENTION!

What you focus on, what you allow within your mind is what you will think about. It is what you will gravitate to, it is what you will internalize with speech and action as well. Imagine why certain companies spend so much money on advertising. They want to persistently get into your mind, to cause you to think about their product. According to a Statista.com review in 2020, media advertising in 2019 in the US was almost 240 billion dollars. If there are approximately 330 million people in the US, that means companies spend approximately $727 per person per year to catch your attention. Over $727 just to catch your attention, to get into your mind, to be in your presence. Why? Because the more their product is pushed into your focus, the more likely you will spend your money on it or act on their message.

Extreme efforts are made by social media, advertisers, news media and entertainment to catch your attention. Millions of dollars are spent on studying the psychological opportunities to grab your attention. We are up against a machine of attention-seeking, behavior-influencing machines to get you to do something, spend money or spend time on what they want you to do. It is indeed a David versus Goliath scenario in regard to a battle for your attention. And the good news is… even though you are one against the Goliath, the machine of attention-hungry entities, you are ultimately in control of it all. You are in control of what you give your attention to, if you choose a design approach. The moment you fall into a default approach, your attention will get sucked into and lost in the labyrinth of an attention-grabbing machine. The time you have is a precious and limited resource. Guard it thusly.

Time Currency

Your attention is valuable. There is a finite amount of time in this life and what we give our attention to could certainly be considered costly in time currency. Advertisers certainly recognize that and spend a lot of money on you to spend your time currency (attention) on their products.

Now time currency can be given freely or frugally. You can spend it by default, wasteful or by design with purpose. The odd thing about time currency is that unlike traditional money currency you never know how much is in the bank. There is no way to gain more or increase our savings account of time. At some point or another, we will all run out of time currency. Now, you can view this as a negative (which after reading through the Positivity section of this book, I hope you do not) or you can view it as a precious thing and use it wisely. Harmon Okinyo is attributed with saying, "Time is a currency you can only spend once, so be careful how you spend it."

What does time currency have to do with thinking? Well, I am glad you asked this question. Your thoughts and your time thinking about something are valuable. What you think about or how you choose to think or focus on is how you choose to spend your time currency. It is how we decide to use it, either by default or by design. What you spend your attention on, your focus is what you meditate on. Sounds odd that you could be meditating on social media, TV, Netflix or something of that nature. But where you give your focus and attention is indeed how you meditate and fill your mind. What you spend your time currency shows what you value. Again, you can think about something intentionally, either by default or design. What is it that you value to invest your time currency?

When you identify what you are investing your time currency on, you can make intentional decisions to remove those things, thoughts, and information out of your sphere that are not positive or beneficial. This is a critical first step in taking control of your THINK. Intentionally decide what you will invest your time currency on. But what do you do now that you have removed your attention away from those negative things, thoughts and information that will not benefit you and others in a positive way?

Earlier we discussed if you remove a thinking process (or attention to something), it is important to replace it with something better and intentionally or, by default, the previous thinking will return to fill the vacuum. Let's work on a practical example of this approach by addressing a focus attention exercise. Words can be powerful in your mind. They can create or destroy opportunity. So, what can we do to fill our minds with positivity now that we have cleared space from those things that are not beneficial to us or others?

Focus Attention: Practical Exercise (1)

Review the short list of words below in the table. Pick one word that has been on your mind lately. A word that describes where your head has been lately. Focus on it, think on it.

Accomplish	Awful	Creative	Lonely	Powerful
Disgusting	Grateful	Useless	Inspired	Terrified
Cheerful	Ugly	Persistent	Narrow	Strength
Intolerant	Willpower	Arrogant	Confident	Clumsy
Excellence	Lazy	Joyful	Rude	Motivated
Stress	Relaxed	Tired	Focused	Frustrated
Happy	Scared	Relieved	Worried	Great
Anxious	Super	Bitter	Fantastic	Angry

Write the word here: _____

Think on three things associated with the word. Now let's apply how this word can have a powerful impact on you.

1. Think on how this word is included in your daily life.
2. Think about where you have read, heard and seen this word in your daily life.
3. Think on how this word, if applied in some capacity, could impact your life.

Realize the power of what you focus on.

The next question is why did you choose the word? Is it because it is something that has been on your mind already? Is it because it related to your current emotional state? The words above are a mix of positive and negative words. Because humans are hard-wired to focus on negative things, I would imagine you picked a negative word or was drawn to one of the negative words in the list. Your mind selected the word that best fit the emotional state you are currently experiencing. This is a default approach to your focus and attention. If you selected a negative word (or perceived negative word), you are more than likely living on the default approach.

Now, let's try another approach to this practical exercise. What if we intentionally picked a positive word from a list of positive words. What if we overrode our current emotional state and intentionally selected a word that has a positive definition or connotation? This is a design approach to your focus and attention. Using the E-Motion approach, you can design how you feel in environments and circumstances as opposed to the environments and circumstances determining your emotion. Remember, using E-Motion is a verb, that's your design approach. Having emotion, as a noun, is when you give up your choice to the environment and circumstances. You have the power to identify what you will want to place your attention. You have the power to investigate that which you place your attention. You have the power to initiate that which you have given your attention.

Focus Attention: Practical Exercise (2)

Review the short list of words below in the table. Pick one, focus on it, think on it.

Accomplish	Wonderful	Creative	Connected	Powerful
Beautiful	Grateful	Useful	Inspired	Pleased
Cheerful	Amazing	Persistent	Focused	Strength
Tolerant	Willpower	Humble	Confident	Graceful
Excellence	Proactive	Joyful	Kind	Motivated
Acclaimed	Relaxed	Beneficial	Focused	Dazzling
Happy	Genuine	Relieved	Beaming	Great
Accepted	Super	Champion	Fantastic	Winner

Write the word here: _____

Think on three things associated with the word. Now let's apply how this word can have a powerful impact on you.

1. Think on how this word is included in your daily life.
2. Think about where you have read, heard and seen this word in your daily life.
3. Think on how this word, if applied in some capacity, could impact your life.

The big difference between the two lists. The first list includes positive and negative words. A real-world example of words we typically encounter and allow into our minds on a regular basis. The second list includes only positive words. A design approach to intentionally choosing what you allow into your mind. The incredible thing about this is that you have the power to pick the list of words in your daily life. You have the power to choose what you give your attention to. E-Motion is the chosen state of mind through intentional thinking.

Let me give you an example of intentional thinking. The other day I had recently completed a project for an organization that involved a lot of work uploading videos, documents, graphics and setting things up in a specific manner. This project was to be made available on desktop and mobile versions. I spent time testing it on the desktop and mobile phone set up for several days. It was completed and ready for rollout. Right before roll-out, my wife was able to test it on her phone. It did not work. I tested again on my phone and it worked. Suddenly it clicked I never tested the mobile version on a different operating system (Android versus iPhone). In that moment, I could have chosen a variety of words to express my feelings. I could have even gotten angry because, after all that work, my wife found a glaring problem.

Here is where my E-Motion kicked in, my THINK had been focused on positivity through this entire process. I looked at this error, mistake or whatever negative word you may want to refer to it as an opportunity. Even though it was something I overlooked and missed during testing, it was an opportunity to learn something new about a different phone operating system, correct it and help other people access the information they may not have been able to access. It turned out to be a win-win. I learned about a new phone system and helped others ensure they could access the project for the organization at the same time. Even in the bigger picture, I learned my wife is great at testing and digging into the details. That is her extraordinary talent and a resource for me for future projects.

Realize the power of intentionally focusing on a positive word and how it can impact your life.   Let's ask another question while focusing on the positive word:

How would you think about overcoming a negative scenario using the positive word you are focused on?

The positive word, the focus you place on it, has the power to overcome even a negative situation. We have a strong bias for negative thinking. It is instinctive. It is our default thinking. We also have the power to choose what we allow.

Now let's continue to focus on the positive words in our leadership world. Review the list of positive words below that relate to positivity in leadership. Identify one of the words you can hold onto that would serve you in your leadership world.

Focus Attention: Practical Exercise (3)

Review the short list of words below in the table. Pick one, focus on it, think on it.

Self-Motivated	Confident	Optimistic	Accountable	Courageous
Engaged	Character	Passion	Integrity	Respectable
Ethical	Loyal	Charismatic	Appreciative	Humility
Disciplined	Perspective	Self-Assure	Mature	Lead-by-Example
Relational	Speaker	Honest	Transparent	Reasonable
Bold	Listener	Authentic	Empowering	Teacher
Inspiring	Visionary	Motivator	Responsible	Rewarding
Coach	Fair	Decisive	Committed	Consistent
Resourceful	Street Smart	Strategic	Proactive	Flexible
Organized	Creative	Intuitive	Curious	Helper

Write your leadership word here:_____

Think on three things associated with the word. Now let's apply how this word can have a powerful impact on you.

1. Think on how this word is included in your leadership.
2. Think about where you have read, heard and seen this word in your career.
3. Think on how this word if, applied in some capacity, could impact your career.

The word or words that you meditate on, that you focus on, that you carry with you will determine your level of success. This again will either happen by default or design. Thoughts are tools for your speak and action. Pick the best tools to create the best results. Put positive thoughts in your tool belt, invest in the right tools. When you buy cheap tools, they don't last long. The same thing with your thoughts; cheap thoughts will not allow you to build the right foundation or create successful scenarios.

Now don't get me wrong, leadership can be stressful. I get it, I have been in various leadership roles for over two decades. There are days in which the stress from leadership can feel overwhelming. I am reminded though through my stressful experiences that we can choose to become a victim of our thoughts or lead them. In one of my earlier leadership roles, I was responsible for several team members and an avalanche of hundreds of students along with their parents and several other family members to get moved into the residence halls at a university within a couple of days.

Preparing a move in for one person can be stressful enough due to all the prep work and paperwork. When you add hundreds and hundreds to that number, it has the potential to become downright end of the world type of stress if you allow it. However, it was then that I was focusing on something positive and so was my team. I did not know it specifically at the time, but I did know enough that if I allowed the stress of the situation to get to me, then it would indeed become an end of the world stress ball. Instead, on that day and for several days following, my team and I chose to focus on the positive potential of the opportunity. And you know what? We got through it.

We learned from it, we excelled at it and we got better at it each year. Sure, we made mistakes here and there, and that was acceptable as long as we kept learning and getting better. We made it through because we intentionally decided to choose to be positive over the negative. We did not allow what seemed to be an impossible circumstance to decide our thinking. A great American philosopher, William James shared, "The greatest weapon against stress is our ability to choose one thought over another." This is the power of your THINK. If you fill your mind with stressful thoughts, words or pictures, then choosing one over another will be extremely difficult because all you can choose from are the negative thoughts, words and pictures that are there. If you fill your mind with positive thoughts, then you have a fighting chance.

What about all the other thoughts that flood our mind every day. Especially those that have nothing to do with leadership. How can we manage and deal with the ones about remembering to add bread to the grocery list or filling up the car with gas? We are constantly in the THINK process. How can you even track the thoughts you have within a day? Some studies have discovered an average person has about 12,000 to 60,000 thoughts in a day. That is a lot of thinking. Well, here is the kicker – of those thoughts 80% were negative and 95% were the same thoughts repeated. Understandably there is a lot of repeated negativity to overcome.

Imagine if you will, you are carrying around a large stack of sticky notes and a pen. For every thought that comes across your mind, you write on a sticky note. When you finish writing the thought on the sticky note, you place it wherever you may be at the very moment.

Imagine you are in the kitchen by the fridge and a thought flashes that you need to buy milk. Ok, write down that thought on the sticky note and place it on the fridge. Moments later you are in the bedroom by your bed and a thought flashes that you need to pay the electric bill and then you think about expensive the electric bill is now. Ok, write them down on the sticky note and place it on the bed. Then you turn around to get your socks from the chest of drawers and another thought flashes that you need to take the trash out before garbage day. There's another sticky note. As you walk to the front door you think about the projects for work today, the commute, the stress from your boss, you forgot to pack your lunch, you need to talk to your neighbor, is it going to rain today, sticky note, sticky note, sticky note.

Continue this throughout the day. Before you leave for work, you would have potentially hundreds, or thousands of sticky notes scattered all through-out the house placed on random things that have no correlation. Like the sticky note in your sock drawer to take out the trash. All the sticky notes would eventually (probably within a week) fill up your house. Random and frustrating. According to research, most of the notes would be negative and repeated. This type of thought process is constantly floating around our minds within a default mindset. Now think about it, would you allow these sticky notes to determine your emotions? Or would your E-Motion determine how you handle a small sticky note?

THINK Key

Interestingly enough, researchers have determined that we can only hold between three to four things on our conscious mind at once. This is the critical information to recognize. Regardless of the thousands and thousands of thoughts you have every day, we work with only three to four at a time. That's three to four sticky notes at a time. We repeat 95% of our thoughts!

This is the secret to it all in the THINK. If we know we can only work with three to four thoughts at a time and we repeat 95% of our thoughts, then pick wisely. What sticky note will you be holding on to? Choose a positive word that you can fill one of the three to four thoughts that you can work with and let that be ingrained in your mind. Immerse yourself with the word, the thought that will serve you beneficially. Internalize what you want to think on. You have great examples provided in this chapter, start by picking one of the words shared or find one that best fits you and then possibly venture out to find the positive word that is right for you. Then secure that sticky note to your forehead and walk proudly around with it on display.

Now that you have your word filling one of the three to four working thoughts, you are ready to move on to initiating the THINK. The foundation of this book, as mentioned before, is filling your mind by design. Your chosen MINDSET is your THINK.

Create a Connection

The THINK you allow will need to be connected to your SPEAK and ACT eventually. Consider the word, the thoughts you choose. Understand the power you have is to choose one thought over another. These thoughts will need to be part of your speech and action. From personal experience, I have chosen thoughts that seemed great in my mind, but when applied to speech and action, it did not feel connected; it did not feel right. It was not what I considered "speakable" and "actionable" in my everyday life. And that is ok. As odd as it sounds, SUPERFANTASTIC was a process to develop for me. It sounded great in my head and I knew if this was the thought that would be my foundational THINK, I would hold onto it as one of the three to four thoughts that I can retain at a time. This would be my sticky note secured to my forehead. Then it had to be "speakable" and "actionable". It took time and courage to say this word, and transform it into my speech and action. It had greater meaning for me. It became forever legitimate after speaking out the name to my mentor as what I wanted to name my first book. This was the THINK that I knew I could connect to my speak and act. Find your THINK that you can connect to your SPEAK and ACT.

LEADERSHIP - THINK

Let's get our leadership THINK on. CEO Alan Mulally, who famously saved both Ford and Boeing, once shared, "The most important discipline a leader can practice is to seek understanding before seeking to be understood." There is a process within this quote. Focus on your THINK before focusing on other's THINK. Understanding is a version of perspective. How do you understand something? You run it through your perspective. If you have a negative perspective, then your understanding will be negative. If you have a positive perspective, then your understanding will be positive. This is the formula we discussed earlier. Here we can apply and initiate the THINK as a leader with the Internal, External and Overall leadership within our THINK.

Have you seen leaders that take the time to understand what is happening prior to making decisions? They ask the team for feedback so that their decisions can be more accurately made. Or the opposite can be true as well. There are some leaders that are able to grasp the current state of the organization and team and based on their insight. Both approaches are effective and can be accurate. However, what is common between both approaches is that both include insight and understanding. One will dive deeper and the other stays on the surface to make their decision. The key for the leader is to gain insight before the decision. Decisions made without insight are doomed to fail. Before insight and decisions are made, it all passes through the leader's perspective to create an understanding that leads to a determined insight.

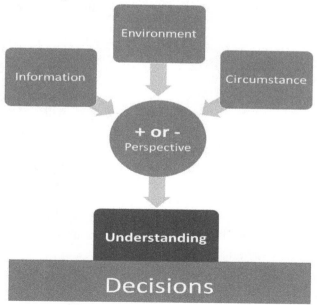

Your think process is your process to gain an understanding not only for yourself, but for others. Ever notice when you focus on a word, a thought or concept, that you begin to see it around you a lot or even the potential of it. An example that a lot of us will be familiar with is when you begin thinking about buying a new car. No matter the brand or color you decide, all of a sudden, that will be the brand and color you begin seeing all around you. This is intentional awareness because it is what you are focused on. Now imagine having a focus or intentional awareness of the positive potential of your organization and team. If you see your organization and team from a negative perspective, then that is what you will find around you. When you begin to see your organization and team in a positive perspective, then that is what you will see. You will begin to see it around you and the potential for more.

Establish what it means to think better, to think as a better leader. What does that mean for you? What does that mean for others? How will others benefit as you begin to intentionally think better as a leader? Identify, Investigate and now Initiate the parameters and measures you will think on to improve your thought process as a leader. Start with you and then share and watch it duplicate through the three components of leadership.

Internal

Remember internal leadership is honoring yourself. Here is the initiation part of THINK. Honor yourself with positive thoughts. Surround yourself with stimuli that will support you in your positive thought process and grow your understanding. It's your sticky note. You have a pen (pick your favorite color) and select the positive word. That is the gift you give yourself as a leader. It is the gift that you will eventually be able to share with others. Use the investigate portion within the previous chapters to assist you in initiating the positive think. This is the foundation of your THINK. Get that sticky note right, secure it to your forehead* and think proudly.

Stick it to your forehead metaphorically but if you want to make the point within your organization and team that you are making a positive change and this is your positive word, then more power to you! You just might start something fun and positive.

External

Once you spend time internalizing internal leadership THINK, you can branch into understanding your team.   Remember understanding your team will filter through your perspective. At this point, it should be a positive perspective. Think of what is important for their success. External leadership is honoring others. By default, many leaders will think of how they can use a person to better their own success. Whereas, by design, a positive thinker will deliberate on how they can identify, investigate and initiate opportunities for their team to be successful. This is where you also encourage your team to think for themselves. When you have a team that can think on their own and make intelligent, business-minded decisions, then your leadership world becomes that much more successful.

Overall

Now you will begin to encourage others to think positively, to meditate on the possible and what can be done as opposed to thinking all things are impossible. Once an individual team member can think on their own, they will be able to support others to make better decisions and think on their own. Overall leadership is duplicating your honor. Your think begins to duplicate itself. Your team begins to train others to think better. They will honor each other through the support and positivity you have established as the foundation and culture within the organization and team. When you see an organization or team walking around with sticky notes on their forehead that have positive words, you are creating success!

Here is the big question I am sure some of you are ready to ask. What is the ROI on THINK? I can sum this up simply. Find me a leader in any capacity that has a THINK focused on negativity within a default mode and a leader that has a THINK focused on positivity within a design mode and I will show you an incredible delta between the success levels between the two. Internalizing a positive design mode THINK into your personal and professional life will create more opportunities than the opposite. Your ROI is the potential ahead of you and just as important the potential of the people around you impacted by your THINK. The mindset you choose either by default or by design will determine your success or failure within this chapter. Leaders with a design mindset understand it is their decision to think on things that are positive and beneficial. They select the thoughts that will allow them to improve themselves and others. They understand the pending connection between what they think and how they will eventually speak and act. The mindset is the foundation of choosing to be a positive thinker. To have positive sticky notes all around.

Initiate: Think *Wrapped Up*

I am SUPERFANTASTIC!	An experiment to start filling your mind with good things.
Time Currency	What you think about is what you value.
Practical Exercise	The word you focus on determines your thoughts.
THINK Key	You have 3-4 spots in your mind to hold a thought. Pick a positive one.
Create a Connection	What you think should be speakable and actionable.
Leadership THINK	Includes understanding of yourself and others.

ACTION & STEPS: Process Planning Notes

Question	Your Thoughts
Identify why you "Think" differently?	
Investigate how you would elevate your "Think"?	
Initiate what would be your "Think"?	

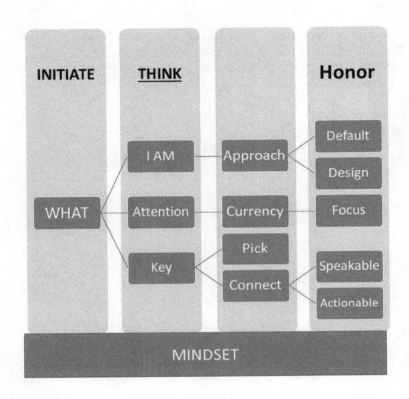

Chapter 4

Initiate: SPEAK

"Let no corrupting talk come out of your mouths, but only such as is good for building up, as fits the occasion, that it may give grace to those who hear."
Ephesians 4:29

Before we begin this chapter, let's continue our in-book experiment now. Read this statement out loud and let the sound of the statement fill the room. Now be mindful if you are reading this book in a public place and say this statement out loud, you might find other people smile when you speak it.

I am SUPERFANTASTIC!

Do not dismiss saying this statement out loud. It may feel weird in the moment but remember you can act your way into a feeling better than you can feel your way into an action. Speak it now, feel it later. I want you to speak this statement again. Re-read this statement out loud at least seven times. And with conviction! If you do not say it with conviction and believe it, then no one will believe it either. Let it roll off your tongue to a point that it becomes easy to say and that you actually believe it. Okay, now that you have participated in the second part of our experiment, we can move on.
We will come back to this later.

Just imagine having a selection of tools that you can put together in certain order and sequences to create some of the most amazing things. Things that could lift up another person, prevent a person from hurting themselves or even make a person cry in joy. We all have access to these tools at our disposal, but it is up to us to use them and sequence them together properly. Words are the tools that give us the ability to do so much. These tools are selected one by one either by default or design. When you choose a tool by default, it may not be the right tool for the job and actually do more harm than good. When you select a tool by design, it will work for the job needed. It will either improve performance or encourage the extra effort needed for the circumstance. Selecting the right tool for the job can make the difference between making things worse or making things better. What is a great way to learn about tools? Through science! Please allow me to share more science, this time word science.

WORD SCIENCE!

Let's look into some science and statistics in regard to words. Remember, I am a bit of a nerd, so I do enjoy the science behind these areas we discuss. Let's start by asking how many words are in the English language. I figured that would be an easy answer, but there are new words entering the lexicon all the time. We create new words as a result of a myriad of factors whether it be through social construct or world events. The English language also likes to adopt words from other languages and embrace them as our own.

But what really is a word? Sounds like a simple question with a simple answer, I mean you have spent a large portion of your life looking at, experiencing and interpreting and inferring words. Breaking it down though, a word is simply a unit of language that carries a meaning. And to boot, each word can come with a family of variations based on how it is used in different tenses. Depending on the area of the country you reside in or visit, there will be versions of words based on dialects. Slang and jargon are additional sources of words to explore. Can you also imagine words that represent sounds? These are the fun words that we get to read in relation to what the sound might sound like spelled out.

Let's break down the number of words in the English language. Again, we introduce new words into the language all the time, so we will only look at a snapshot in time of the number of words. In 2010 Google estimated there to be over 1 million words and that it would grow by several thousand each year. I imagine you know and possibly use several words that have entered into your vocabulary in recent years.

If there are so many words in the English language, how many words does an average person know? According to Robert Charles Lee in his publication in Quora, he shared that about 3,000 words will cover 95% of everyday writing. Of those 3,000 words, the first 1,000 are used in 89% of everyday writing. Most adult native speakers will range from 20,000-35,000 words according to The Economist based on test results from TestYourVocab.com.

Get this, according to the Linguistic Society of America, as recently as 2009 there are about 6,909 distinct languages in the world noted from the Ethnologue. Here are some words facts from BestLifeOnline.com to increase your knowledge of words:

1. The longest English word is nearly 190,000 letters (happens to be a protein chemical name). — *Would like to see that on the nutrition label on some jar.*

2. There is a word for all things breakfast: jentacular. — *Certainly, my favorite meal of the day and now, word of the day.*

3. A single piece of confetti is called a "confetto". — *Sounds like a sad party celebration.*

4. There is a word to refer to the day before yesterday: nudiustertian. — *Feels like a four-score and some days ago word.*

5. The English word "set" has the most meanings of any word. — *How many meanings can you identify without looking them up?*

Would you be surprised to know that the word "the" is the most commonly used word in the English language? It is a powerful word and one that I recommended to use when describing your role or what you do instead of "just".

Now let's get into speaking facts. The words are there to fill our minds and now it is up to us to choose to speak the words we speak. Most average people can speak about 100-130 words per minute. Now if you are like me, I want to know who spoke the most words in a minute. That would be Steve Woodmore. This retired British comedian could speak up to 637 words per minute. Talk about getting tongue-tied.

Finally speaking of getting tongue-tied. We can close out word science with the part of the body that has a lot to do with getting the words out. Our tongue consists of eight muscles and is a small part of the body, but so very powerful. I believe Charles R. Swindoll shared it well with, "We need to think of our tongue as a messenger that runs errands for our heart. Our words reveal our character." Our tongue gives life or death to the things we are thinking of. Our tongue manifests our thoughts.

WORDY ATTENTION

Your SPEAK is where the world can hear what you have created in your mind and what your character reveals. Now remember, everyone has their own perception of what they hear. Your words may mean one thing to you and something totally different to another person. This can prove challenging when in your mind you feel and understand what you think and speaking the thoughts form your mind are taken a different way. As you have a perception filter either negative or positive, everyone else has a similar perception filter. What you speak is information they will process through their own filter. That is the opportunity in it all. If your THINK and SPEAK are positive, constructive and supportive, then you are on the right path. Keep thinking and speaking those things that are positive, constructive and supportive and their filter will begin to clear up as you continue to focus your attention and words on these things. Others will begin to adjust their perception and filter as they see the good or success coming from your SPEAK.

Be intentional about your think and speak for others to see and hear your value. If you are thinking one thing, word or thought and then speak something different, it makes it even more difficult for others to believe and accept you. Intentional speaking comes in two forms: default and design. A default intentional speaker will allow anything on their mind to be said. There is little constructive or positive value from their words, it is more for the leader to hear themselves talk. The words get clumped into meaningless gibberish or even self-promotion from the default intentional speaker. On the flip side, the design intentional speaker will share words that have meaning and purpose. It is not that this type of speaker will filter every word, but as their think has become positive and their focus to be constructive and support becomes internalized, then the words of value will find their way. You may already know this, but your words have value and show what you value.

Speak Currency

As mentioned before, what you say reveals what you value. Speaking words to your organization or team that have value will create value for you as a leader. What are the things that you can speak as a design intentional speaker to show what you value as a leader and what you value from your organization and team? Below are a handful of phrases that will peak the attention of your organization and team when the leader speaks. These are the currency of what you value in your words. Make these phrases your own in your leadership conversations with your organization and team:

Let me be transparent. When a leader is transparent it prevents things or situations from being hidden. Organizations and teams want to know what is happening. They do not want to feel left out or feel like there will be a surprise around every corner. When a leader speaks to transparency, it provides the organization and team with a feeling of trust and being valued as someone that should know. That they have the interest to know what is going on. Transparency is a cure for gossip and misunderstandings.

Our next step will be... In the spirit of being transparent, the organization and team also value understanding what the next step is and how they can prepare and take the next steps to be part of the solution and or success. This gives visibility into the future and guidance to the steps that will be taken to continue moving forward and upward.

What can I do to support you? It can be difficult for some team members to ask for help, others may find it very easy. Regardless of their level of need for support, it is always nice to know that your leader is willing to support you on some level. Knowing it is one thing, but hearing the words spoken from your leader directly to you is in some cases as valuable as actually receiving support directly. Be prepared to help if asked. Be prepared to follow up and follow through with requests for support.

What else should I know? Contrary to what some leaders think, leaders do not know everything. They should depend on their organization and team to fill in the gaps of information. Don't assume there is nothing else to know. Asking your organization or team this question creates a sense of trust in that person. If you value the organization and team, then you trust to get their feedback on what else needs to be known. Remember only to ask this question when you are ready to hear an answer. And do something with the information you receive.

Let's decide based on our core values. If you have a set of core values in place, then this should be your guiding light when making decisions. Your organization and team should know and understand that the core values of the company are of value and not empty words. When a leader defers to making decisions based on the company core values, the organization and team can feel the value of how the company operates and will remain steady and tied to a set of values. This creates a level of comfort and confidence. If there are not a set of core values at your company, make this happen.

You have my trust. As important as the words "what can I do to support you" can feel, this phrase is the ultimate in building up an organization and team. When a leader values a team member and shares this phrase it gives the team member autonomy and responsibility to be free to make choices on behalf of the company. This is empowering for an organization and team. Trust is a valuable commodity and should be issued with empowerment and guidance. Giving someone room to work within the grey can be overwhelming for some.

Let's learn and grow through this. As much as autonomy and responsibility are valued when trust is given, so is support. We make mistakes. It is expected. The only time you know when a team member is not working is when they are never making mistakes. When your organization or team hears this, they recognize and value that it is acceptable to make mistakes. That does not mean there is no accountability. The accountability part stems from learning and growing better because of the mistake, not in spite of it.

Congratulations! Finally, when the time is right, and you have a specific reason this word is golden to your organization and team. You have accomplished your goal, your mission or reached a milestone, do not forget to celebrate the wins.

As valuable as these phrases can be for a leader, there are instances in which a design intentional speaker should not speak. This is an absolute must to grasp. When it comes to gossip, a design leader should refrain at all cost. Gossip is of no value and in turn, will dissolve trust. Should you hear gossip, the only words a design intentional speaker should share is, "let's speak to the person you are speaking about and address it directly with that person." That is it. Gossip within an organization or team is a killer. There is no benefit from gossip or passive-aggressive speaking in any capacity about another person.

These words (or lack thereof) are the phrases that have value to the person on the other side. Your words are currency similar to the deposits we make into the appreciation bank accounts. Be prepared to spend these words and phrases daily. Remember only to ask the questions when you are ready to hear an answer.

Connect What Is Disconnected

This is the first opportunity to start making connections within the THINK, SPEAK, ACT process. You are spending proper time creating the environment to fill your mind with positive thoughts and words. Now is the time to support the journey of your thoughts out into the world.

If what you think is different than what you speak it will self-sabotage your outcome. If you are thinking positive thoughts, opportunities and goals, and out of your mouth comes negative words or doubt, then you will rarely meet your potential. It is important to make the connection between your thoughts and speech. Let's get the connection right with a second practical exercise.

SPEAK It: Practical Exercise

Review the short list of words below in the table. Pick the word that you chose in THINK and speak it out loud.

Self-Motivated	Confident	Optimistic	Accountable	Courageous
Engaged	Character	Passion	Integrity	Respectable
Ethical	Loyal	Charismatic	Appreciative	Humility
Disciplined	Perspective	Self-Assure	Mature	Lead-by-Example
Relational	Speaker	Honest	Transparent	Reasonable
Bold	Listener	Authentic	Empowering	Teacher
Inspiring	Visionary	Motivator	Responsible	Rewarding
Coach	Fair	Decisive	Committed	Consistent
Resourceful	Street Smart	Strategic	Proactive	Flexible
Organized	Creative	Intuitive	Curious	Helper

Write your leadership word here: _____

Speak it to yourself. Share it with an alignment or mentor. Allow your alignment or mentor to help you with the word and ask questions. If you cannot "defend" or support the word that you will allow yourself to think on and speak out loud, then it's time to find another word. Let it resonate with you when you speak it out loud. Say it to yourself in the mirror if that helps. Can you picture yourself say this word out loud to others? Let's start making a connection. Did the word you chose in THINK feel right when you spoke it out loud? This may take a few tries to get it. Think it and speak it out loud. Do it again.

If you feel a disconnect or something does not feel right, go back to the THINK Focus Attention: Practical Exercise (3) and pick another word and go through this again. When you find the right word, it will feel right to think it and speak it out loud. This is a critical connection to make in the process.

Think on three things associated with the word. Now let's apply how this word can have a powerful impact on you and others.

1. How can you speak this word as a leader?
2. Where have you spoken or heard this word in your career?
3. If you spoke this word, how would it impact your career?

The words you speak can have a lasting impression not only for yourself, but for others. What do you remember when you speak? What do other people remember when you speak? Once a word is spoken, it cannot be unspoken. The power of words can be immeasurable. Words can be an effect or create an affect. In a default approach, many times words are spoken as an effect of a circumstance. These words are a result of what has happened or what the environment is at the time. It is simply a reaction. However, words can also be spoken to affect the circumstance through a design approach. No matter the circumstance or environment, words can be a positive impact if you proactively use the right ones. The spoken word is the energy you give to the situation. Let it be energy that creates opportunity and positivity. What you speak is what you will find, it becomes part of your perception.

How do we create the energy from our SPEAK as a leader? You have the ability to create E-Motion with your speak. Remember that E-Motion is a chosen state of mind creating one's circumstance, mood, or relationship with others. To create E-Motion with your speak, you will need to choose the words that will create the mood or relationship you desire to create. When you speak negative words, that is what you will create. When you speak positive, constructive and meaningful words, that is what you will begin to create. Not only are the words you speak important, the way or method in which you speak them is important as well. Now I am not going to get into a long conversation about public speaking, I simply want to create awareness of the initiation of your speaking. Let's look at two of the main components of your speaking to create E-Motion.

Passion is proof that you believe in what you are speaking. If you do not believe in what you are saying, then no one else will either. It is acceptable for a leader to believe in what they are saying and say it with excitement. Now I am not saying that you need to scream or jump up and down when speaking to your organization or team, but an amount of energy, belief and excitement should come across while you are speaking. You should have conviction in your words and the way you speak them.

Engagement will bring your team into your message. This is the method in which you get your organization and team to lean in while you are speaking. Your passion will create a sense of engagement. Knowing your organization and team and what's important to them helps. Be with your organization and team when speaking. Your words include a variation of "us" and "we" are in this together approach. The leader and the organization and team are all on the same side.

If the spoken word has such power, what about other forms of communication. Let's talk about other ways in which you can speak. In the traditional sense, the spoken word would be considered your speak. I would also like for you to consider another powerful format for speak or communication. That would include written words. Both have equal power on their own.

What is a **Written** word? It is simply your thoughts transformed into energy either on paper or on a screen. These words become sentences and sentences become your action. That eventually becomes your calling card. Emails, text and other forms of social media have created new ways to speak your thoughts. It seems that emojis and gifs have also become acceptable forms of communication at certain levels, even in the business world. Depending on your work environment, I would though, caution against extensive use of emojis and gifs as a formal format for your follow-up memos. In all of the forms of the written word, it is certainly important to remember that emotion can be difficult to send through the written word. Unless of course, you send your message in all caps.

You will not find a course here on how to write, I struggle enough with that myself. What I would like to impart with you is when writing to your organization and team, use the positive words from your think and include your speak currency to convey your message. Your organization and team will appreciate the format.

Goldilocks Portion

I mention a lot of speaking and writing positivity as a leader. My next question to pose is how much should you speak and write? When is it enough or too little or just right? Feels like we should spend a moment discussing and understanding the proper portion amounts of speaking and writing that are just right. What better way to help visualize this approach than our favorite storybook person that loves to compare things, Goldilocks. Goldilocks found porridge too hot, too cold and just right. She found a chair too hard, too soft and just right and finally found three beds to compare as well. Goldilocks knew what she liked after making a few comparisons.

Find your levels of comparison as well when considering speaking and writing. Know your audience and capacity for their attention. Know the subject and the necessity of the portion of words needed. Uncover the cadence and tempo of your words. The Goldilocks Portion is the right amount to connect with the audience and with the message. Know there are times in which your words should be short and sweet or lengthy. Understanding when to keep it short or when to extend, is a valuable tool as a leader. Sometimes silence is a proper portion as well.

Some leaders are able to find the sweet spot in as few words as possible. President George Washington in his inaugural address spoke 135 words, short enough to be a tweet. However, on the flip side, Krishna Menon spoke for eight hours in 1957 in front of the UN Security Council. Now that is not to say what Krishna Menon spoke was not powerful or eloquent or equally important, it is to point out that you should know your message, your audience and connect the two. So how long should your speech be to your organization and team? And the short answer is, it depends. It depends on how long you can hold your organization and team's attention; how long will it take to impactfully deliver your message and, of course, the logistics of your organization and team needing to get back to work.

The Goldilocks Portion is certainly not an exact science, but through practice, working with your alignments and mentors including understanding the impact of the message, you will start to develop a more refined Goldilocks Portion to best convey your speak. With all of the components of speak to initiate, it is important to remember it will take time to continue to develop your speak.   Filling your mind with positive words, then connecting this to your speak is the first manifestation of who you are as a leader.

LEADERSHIP - SPEAK

As a leader, what you say has the ability to form beliefs and values of how your team sees their worth as a team member and person.   When you choose to speak, use words that are specific to the occasion and will build others up.   Let others understand that the words from you, as their leader, are meant for correction and support. Words can offer hope and grace to those that need your affirmation in times of stress and trouble. The power of a leader's speak can be immeasurable to a person. I can still hear specific statements and words from my previous leaders that resonate with me today.   Examples like, "Inspect what you expect," "Create a sense of urgency," "Don't assume and ask questions" and so many others.   These words helped shape how I became a leader over the years. Speak to yourself and others with positive intentions. Those words can last.

Ever notice that when you speak something, you will begin to see it around you?   For example, when you hear a catchphrase and you begin to add it to your vocabulary you will hear it said by everyone else.   I certainly do not want to age myself and share the catchphrases that I am "hip" to, but you get the point.   This is intentional awareness.   Leaders have the influence to create catchphrases within their organization and team.   Ever heard, "my pleasure..."?   That is a powerful catchphrase used at a large organization and it makes a positive difference.

When you begin to formulate your speak and share words that are constructive, positive and meaningful, you will eventually hear your organization and team use the same as well. It becomes a catchphrase.   In the absence of the intentional positive, meaningful or constructive catchphrase, your organization or team will fill in the gap with their own. This is the big difference between default and design speak. The default speak leader will allow their teams to create their own catchphrase and it may not always be what you hoped. A design speak leader will fill the air with the intentional positive, meaningful and constructive words that give the organization and team something to grasp and be "hip" to in their own speak. As much as trends change and become innovative over time, it is the leader's responsibility to continue to update and improve their own speak to keep their organization and team inspired. A leader starting a conversation or speech with "Four score and two quarters ago..." may not inspire much.

Develop what it means to speak better, to speak as a better leader. What does that mean for you? What does that mean for others? Identify, Investigate and now Initiate the parameters and measures you will speak on to improve your words as a leader. Connect it with your thinking. Start with you and then share and watch it duplicate through the three components of leadership.

Internal

Remember internal leadership is honoring yourself. This is the initiation part of SPEAK. Honor yourself with positive words. Surround yourself with alignments, books, media and conversations that will support you through positive, encouraging and challenging words that boost your process and grow your understanding of what to speak. Use the investigate portion within the previous chapters to assist you in initiating the positive speaking. This is the foundation of your SPEAK. Get your words for you right.

External

Once you spend time internalizing internal leadership SPEAK, you can branch into understanding your team. What words are their appreciation language? Speak on what is important for their success. External leadership is honoring others. By default, many leaders will speak to others so that they do what they are told and not as the leader does. Whereas by design a positive speaker will speak on how they can support opportunities for their team to be successful. This is where you encourage your team to speak up as the leader they can become. When you have a team that can speak as a positive leader, then your leadership world will inspire positive growth.

Overall

Now you will begin to encourage others to speak positively to others with positive possibility and what can be done as opposed to thinking all things are impossible. Once an individual team member can speak to others on their own in a leadership fashion, they will be able to support others to speak in authority. Overall leadership is duplicating your honor. Your positive leadership speaking begins to duplicate itself. Your team begins to train others to speak as a leader and in authority. They will honor each other through the support and positivity you have established as the foundation and culture within the organization and team.

Now that your think and speak are building momentum, what does it all mean? What is your ROI on Speak? Just like in the THINK chapter, this can be added up simply. Find me a leader that speaks negatively, and I will show you an organization and team that runs on fear and is far from being committed. In fact, I would share that most employees are there for only the paycheck or looking for a way out. Positive speaking is the manifestation of a leader's thoughts. This is the first set of proofs that the organization and team will see what their leader is made of. Speaking in a positive design manner will create greater successes through building a culture of I CAN and I WILL be better and do better. The ROI of Speak can be the difference between having a successful team or a team checked out or on the way out.

Your words become tools to convey your thoughts to others. Your tools are what you use in order to improve or break things down. The right tool for the right job is an effective way of improvement. For example, you would not use a hammer to fix a computer (although it sometimes is very tempting on occasion), you would use the right word to encourage and support an organization or team. Strung together the tools you have at your disposal through your positive thinking is your toolbox for building up and giving grace to others.

Initiate: Speak *Wrapped Up*

I am SUPERFANTASTIC	An experiment to start speaking good things to yourself.
Word Science	"The" is more powerful than "just".
Speak Currency	Speak to catch attention.
Connect What Is Disconnected	Self-sabotage happens when the think and speak are not aligned.
Speak It: Practical Exercise	The word you think should be the word you are confident to speak.
Goldilocks Portion	Know what and when and how long you should speak for your audience.
Leadership SPEAK	Speak well to others and watch others speak well to others.

ACTION & STEPS: Process Planning Notes

Question	Your Thoughts
Identify why you "Speak" differently?	
Investigate how would you elevate your "Speak"?	
Initiate what would be your "Speak"?	

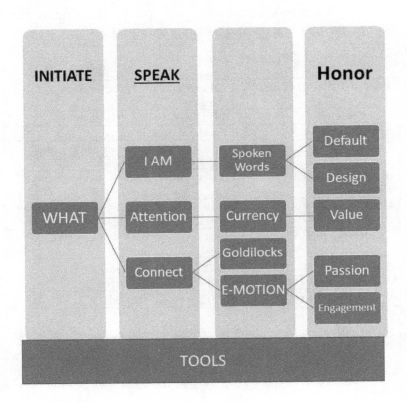

Chapter 5

Initiate: ACT

"But someone will say, 'You have faith and I have works.' Show me your faith apart from your works, and I will show you my faith by my works." James 2:18

We think of many wonderful things. We speak many wonderful things. If we allow it. After working through the conversations for positivity, leadership, setting the foundation for your think and manifesting your thoughts through speak, it is now time for you to act. The think and speak are not enough on its own. Without this final piece, everything else becomes empty unfulfilled promises. Charles D. Gill expressed it perfectly with "There are many wonderful things that will never be done if you do not do them." Let's get ready to go do these many wonderful things that can make a positive difference for you and others.

Before we move into the initiation part of our ACT, we can discuss a little about action. ACT is a commitment to our thoughts and words. When these three items line up you become a messenger of consistency and trustworthiness. Your action becomes the template for what you deem acceptable to your organization and team. As a leader, your organization and team will identify what you deem acceptable and for the most part, adopt it as their own levels or boundaries. People watch you, and as a leader, they watch you closely. Become who you want your organization and team to become.

Choosing to stay committed to what you think and speak will connect the pieces of the process as you initiate. Let's dig into what it means to act. I have heard that you should act first, or just do it, or make things happen. In fact, I believe in a quote that seems contradictory to the order of this process. It goes,

"Acting your way into a feeling is more powerful than feeling your way into an action." If this is the case, then why is ACT after THINK? Shouldn't we skip the think and move on to action? Seems like a waste of time, doesn't it? Glad you are asking these questions. And I want to answer you with a big and emphatic NO!

A lot of what you see in advertisements or social media regarding acting first is based on acting on a feeling. The reason acting on a feeling is bad is because feelings can change. Feelings can be misleading. Feelings stem from a reaction to something. That's emotion, not E-Motion. Emotions are a default approach to acting whereas E-Motion is a design approach to acting. I want to strongly encourage you to not act on feelings or in a default manner when it comes to leadership. When you create a process by which you internalize a thinking process that is positive, constructive and supportive and you follow it with a speaking process that mirrors your think, then your act will have a guide or design approach to follow. You will be less inclined to react. You can and will be proactive with E-Motion. You can and will affect and become the effect of a circumstance or situation.

Feelings are the effect of something and that sets up a default action. I am not saying feelings are bad, on the contrary, as a leader it is important to know the difference between acting with feelings and acting through your thought process. Feelings have their time and place and it is valuable to know when and where. Acting in design fashion is the process of being proactive and creating the affect for the circumstance or situation. You can certainly do it, so long as it is supported by your think and speak. Actions are how we value what we think and speak.

ACTION SCIENCE!

Before we jump into action as a leader, please allow me to share more of my nerdy side with additional science and facts information. A leader can make a lot of strategic moves in the board room, but it is the everyday actions that we take with our organization and team that can create an even more positive outcome. Let's investigate the actions that a typical leader could take in a day.

When you walk the talk, a leader (or average person for that matter) will take between 3,000 to 4,000 steps per day. – *since you are no average person, I can imagine you would have double the steps.*

Getting your message out to your team is important as a leader and a typical one can type out 40 words per minute or 2,400 words per hour. That is a lot of typing. – *gives a new understanding that the meeting could have been an email.*

Burning the midnight oil as a leader can be common, however, at rest, our muscles burn around 8.5 calories per hour. As stress increases so does the heart rate and calories burned. – *stress is certainly not a wise weight loss strategy.*

Sitting at your desk catching up on emails and making phone calls is a common occurrence for a leader. The average person spends 6.5 hours a day sitting. That surely leaves little time to walk around and spend time within the organization and team. – *get up and go mingle, you are no average leader.*

These are a lot of average science facts to share and as mentioned before, you are not average. Understand the average action a regular person takes, and act better than that. Checking off completed tasks from your checklist is certainly a move in the right direction but there is more to it as a leader. Acting out what you have filled your mind with and spoken to your organization and team is action in a whole new way. Your organization and team will see you in action and understand the template for how to make the right moves.

ACT-TENTION

What is it that you do all day? What are the small actions and larger moves you make throughout a day? Where you spend your time acting or moving shows what you value. What projects or tasks you perform are what your organization and team see as the most important projects and tasks for them to address. A leader's role is to spend time acting on the projects, tasks or events that mean the most to the organization and team as a whole. What you act on is where you place your attention or said in another way, this is your ACT-TENTION.

I have experienced leaders spending time acting on so-called pet projects that have very little meaning to the overall benefit of the organization or team. I have seen some leaders spend more time coming up with ideas and little time developing or creating plans to make one of the many ideas work. Other times I have experienced leaders spend their action prioritizing and planning out the ideas and projects that are to best benefit the organization and team. There is a need certainly for spending your time acting on a variety of different components of the process, but there is also a critical need to balance it all. A leader can certainly be busy through action. However, is the leader truly productive through their busy action? A busy leader may be doing and or working on several different projects, reports and tasks. The question that a leader should ask is how is this meaningful or, better yet, productive to elevate the organization and team to the next level? A productive team may have fewer projects or tasks, but they are meaningful and have the potential for greater success. You can choose to do a lot of things good or choose to do a few things great. The attention you give to your action is what the organization and team will eventually give their attention and action. What you act on is initiating value to that specific project, plan or task.

Act Currency

The things that you do as a leader have meaning. As a leader, your time becomes precious due to all of the additional responsibilities that are being added to your plate. So, each act should be done intentionally and efficiently, right? You are busy, there are meetings, emails, reports and phone calls to make. The days fly by as you sit at your desk typing away, running from one meeting to another and finally making it back to your desk just in time to write up another report. Your too busy to stop and spend time with your team. There is never enough time to get things done.

Well, yes you are busy but are you productive? You are in control of your time (for the most part). When everything is a priority, nothing is a priority. When you have more than three to four priorities, you no longer have a priority list you simply have a to-do list. Identify the methods in which you can become efficient and effective. Remember busy can kill productivity. What are ways to initiate productivity within your busy world? Let's explore a few major options.

Delegate to your team in order to multiply your abilities. I understand that numerous leaders will think that it is easier and faster for me to just do it myself. For the longest time, I agreed with that statement and lived that way as a leader until I got called out on it by my own leader. I was burned out and frazzled. It was selfish of me to act that way. If I never delegate, then my organization and team will never have the opportunity to grow. As a leader, I never realized the potential of my team.

When delegating, it is imperative that you **communicate clearly** the objective, task and or goal. Spending time upfront clearly communicating what the steps, tasks and expectations of the delegated project or task are, will save time during and after. Communicate clearly as well, that you believe your team can do it and do it well. Doing it right the first time, which may take a little extra time than rushing through it, will prevent doubling up efforts on the back end doing it again or fixing the mistakes.

Now that your organization has been delegated to and communicated clearly the objective, task and or goal, do they have the **tools** to do it well? What good is making all the preparations to complete a project, task or goal without the means to do so. Tools can come in a variety of forms. Most will think of a tool as something to use. I would also encourage you to think of a tool as the freedom to make decisions and act, and the support needed as they are going through the task or project. These tools can make a difference between stalling out a project or giving the organization a clear path to move ahead.

Once you as the leader, build and go through this process, get **feedback**. You are only as good as your last mistake. Your team is in the trench for you, and with you, fighting the battles for wins and successes. Their perspectives will vary from yours. They will see things that you cannot see. Spending time identifying, investigating the feedback will provide the information to initiate new and better ways for the next project, goal or task.

Intentional actions give you the focus to get through what needs to be done as a leader. When you are mindful of what needs to be accomplished, then you can make moves in that manner.   Intentional actions also include recognizing and acknowledging others in a way that is intentional and meaningful and most importantly, specific.

Up until now, you have been writing leadership checks with your thoughts and speech. Now it is time to cash it in. Let yourself and others reap the benefits of payday. By payday, I mean acting on what your think and speak have been conveying. This is where you connect the first two parts of the process with your ACT. What you ACT is the payday of your THINK and SPEAK. If connected well, everyone can get paid a fortune!

Connect What Is Disconnected

Get ready to do what you have thought and spoken. It is not enough to think and speak positive thoughts and positive words. To make a positive difference it takes actions that align with your thoughts and speech. I am sure you have heard the famous saying, "do as I say, not as I do." Hearing this from a leader can be the most deflating phrase uttered. How do you follow someone that says one thing and does another?

Followable leadership comes from a leader that can connect the THINK, SPEAK and ACT. It is intentional development to create a process through internal leadership into external leadership and ultimately into overall leadership. Making the connection is where you create for yourself the template to live out your personal and professional life. It may seem elementary, but I promise you it is more impactful than you will ever imagine, until you make it happen. Say what you see in your mind so you can act what you say. So, let's get the connection right with the final exercise.

ACT It: Practical Exercise

Review the short list of words below in the table. Pick one and act it out.

Self-Motivated	Confident	Optimistic	Accountable	Courageous
Engaged	Character	Passion	Integrity	Respectable
Ethical	Loyal	Charismatic	Appreciative	Humility
Disciplined	Perspective	Self-Assure	Mature	Lead-by-Example
Relational	Speaker	Honest	Transparent	Reasonable
Bold	Listener	Authentic	Empowering	Teacher
Inspiring	Visionary	Motivator	Responsible	Rewarding
Coach	Fair	Decisive	Committed	Consistent
Resourceful	Street Smart	Strategic	Proactive	Flexible
Organized	Creative	Intuitive	Curious	Helper

Write your leadership word here: _____

Act it out to yourself. Share it (and even act it) with an alignment or mentor. Let it resonate with you when you act it out. Act it out to yourself in the mirror if that helps. Can you see yourself acting this word out to others? Let's start making a connection. Did the word you chose in THINK and SPEAK, feel right when you acted it out? This may take a few tries to get it. Think it and speak it out loud and act it out. Do it again.

If you feel a disconnect or something does not feel right, go back to the THINK Focus Attention: Practical Exercise (3) and pick another word and go through this process again. When you find the right word, it will feel right to think it and speak it out loud and act it. This is the final connection to make in the process.

Think on three things associated with the word. Now let's apply how this word can have a powerful impact on you and others.

1. How can you act this word as a leader?
2. Where have you acted or seen this word acted out in your career?
3. If you acted this word, how would it impact your career?

Become aware of the things you do through self-awareness. There are a lot of movements, actions we take, that have become so internalized that we don't realize that we are doing them. For example, some people will tap their toe when nervous or click the pen top over and over again. Some will avoid eye contact or hold their head down when speaking or repeat the dreaded word "umm" over and over again. These traits can distract your team from your message or even give clues to your true hidden intentions. Connecting what is disconnected is powerful and includes all the little things that could disconnect your think, speak and act through the small body language "quirks" we all have.

What is **Body Language**? It is the process by which a person emphasizes or distracts from what is being spoken or the message being conveyed. This is something that you should be conscious about, but not too conscious. I know that is a weird statement to make and hear me out. The way you present yourself when speaking can become part of the message in a way that will either support the message or punish it. For the most part, we have all heard of body language and the different stances and contortions of your body that impact a message. So again, I will not go into a lesson on that. What I do want to discuss is initiating it.

When speaking a message to your organization or team in person or video, they are watching you as much as they are listening. As much as you should repeat your thinking positive, and speaking positive, you should internalize what your body language looks like while speaking. It should feel and look like a positive action. Practice this from top to bottom.

Here is a fun exercise, video yourself speaking a prepared speech and a casual conversation you would have with a team member. Notice the differences between the two. Notice how you are presenting yourself. Now comes the best part of checking yourself - turn off the volume and watch your actions between the two speeches. If you are not inspired alone by your actions (your body language) then your message will likely get lost. Granted there are some messages that require stoic and uber-professional mannerisms, and there are times in which your body language needs to emphasize a positive message.

Watch it and identify your manners, your movements and dare I say, tics. Do it again on the video. Watch other speakers, leaders and notice their body language. What works, what doesn't. Ask a trusted alignment for feedback. Knowing can help you intentionally work through these nuances that could distract your organization or team from your message.

LEADERSHIP - ACT

As a leader, your actions can make or break apart an organization or team. Understand that what you act on is a reflection for others (including yourself) if they can trust you completely. When I mention trust in this sense, can they trust you to make a positive difference not only for the organization and team, but for them as a person individually? William James, an American Philosopher shared, "Act as if what you do makes a difference. It does."

If you believe in what you think and speak as a leader, then your works will result in a positive and successful outcome. How you ACT becomes proof of the things you think and speak. Your organization and team will hear what you speak and prove it by how you act. Organizations and teams look for examples to follow. For the most part, they will look to the leader and then to their peers for examples on how to act. When a leader is creating followable examples, then the organization and team will have a template by which to act. Both will know what is acceptable and what is not acceptable. A leader must avoid at all cost saying one thing and acting a different way. This creates confusion and divisiveness within the organization and team. Your expectations of yourself should mirror what you expect from your team as well, if not more.

I once had a leader that expected us to go above and beyond for our guests. These were not simple words for her, she exemplified them daily. Every time she would visit our office, she would pick up any trash she saw in the parking lot and bring it in to throw away. She would walk the office area to make sure things were clean and situated appropriately so that we looked our best. If a guest came into the office, we would all stop what we were doing in order to assist the guest. If we got busy, it was not uncommon for her to get behind a desk and assist a customer with their needs. This was the leadership example we wanted to follow. Her words and actions were consistent so that we all knew, even when she was not around those were the expectations for all of us, and we did them. We were successful because we saw our leader act out what she spoke out.

Deploy what it means to act better, to intentionally act as a better leader. What does that mean for you? What does that mean for others? Identify, Investigate and now Initiate the parameters and measures you will act on to improve your action as a leader. Connect it with your thinking and speaking. Start with you and share it with them and watch it duplicate through the three components of leadership.

Internal

Remember internal leadership is honoring yourself. Here is the initiation part of ACT. Honor yourself with positive actions. Immerse yourself with positive examples that will support you through positive, encouraging and challenging actions that boost your process and grow your understanding of what to act as a leader. Do you act as a positive leader within your own home or around your friends? Who are the leaders that you are surrounding yourself with? Are you learning how other positive leaders act and try to emulate for yourself? Are you looking to create transformational encounters with others as practice? What you act in private will become what you act in public. It will become who you are as a person and as a leader. The private "you" and the public "leader you" should be consistent. Use the investigate portion within the previous chapters to assist you in initiating the positive actions. This is the foundation of your ACT.

External

Once you spend time internalizing internal leadership ACT, you can branch into understanding your team. Do your actions fulfill their appreciation language? Do your actions match up with your words of encouragement? Act so that there is a clear progression and support for their success. Act as if what you do makes a difference. External leadership is honoring others. By default, many leaders will act towards others, so it is based on fear and task-driven. Whereas a by design positive act leader will take action to support opportunities for their team to be successful. Are you creating followable excellence in your environment? This is where you encourage your team to act as the positive leader they can become. When you have a team that can take action as a positive leader, then your leadership world will inspire positive growth.

Overall

Duplicating your actions becomes the example for others to follow. You will begin to encourage others to act positively toward others. The possibility of acting as a positive leader for your team creates more opportunities for them. Positive leaders will provide trust and confidence in others to take the right action based on your examples.   Once an individual team member can act as a positive leader towards others, they will be able to support others to act as the leader they can become. Overall leadership is duplicating your honor. Your positive leadership actions begin to duplicate. Your team begins to train others to act as a leader and with encouragement and positivity. They will honor each other through the support and positivity you have established as the foundation and culture within the organization and team.

What is your ROI on Act? As in the SPEAK chapter, we can calculate it out fairly simple. Find me a leader that acts negatively or acts counter to how he or she speaks, and I will show you an organization and team that does not trust or believe in their leader. In addition, it would not be out of the ordinary for the organization and team to do their own thing no matter what the leader speaks or acts. Acting as a leader is proof of what you think and speak to yourself and others. This is how your organization and team can cash in your leadership check. It will either bounce or it will provide everyone with a leadership payday. Acting with the intention that follows the thinks and speak positive approach will generate more than a positive outcome, it will start building a culture. Acting in a positive design manner will create greater successes through building a culture of I DID IT better today than I did yesterday. And I WILL do it better tomorrow than I did today. The ROI of ACT can be the difference between having a culture of belief and trust or not.

Before we end this chapter, let's act on part three of our in-book experiment. How will you act on a powerful statement? Well, this will be on you. You have now filled your mind with a lot of positivity. You have spoken positivity to and about yourself. These words below are now in your mind and spoken out loud to the world.

I am SUPERFANTASTIC!

Here is where you get to create your own experiment and outcome. When you are faced with a task, think this statement again, say this statement again and begin to act on addressing or resolving whatever it is that you are faced with at the moment. Remember, you are SUPER inside so you can create the FANTASTIC outside. Okay, now that you have participated in the third part of our in-book experiment, you have a formula to make this your own. Use this experiment as a process to continue the THINK, SPEAK, ACT approach. If you think it, then you will say it and then ultimately act it. Your word should fit into this experiment. Whatever the positive word you choose in the Practical Exercises, that is your "I am" thought, speech and action. Your word should be connected now in your THINK, connected to your SPEAK and now connected in your ACT. Fill it in and try it now.

"I am [fill in the blank with your positive word]."

This what you get to think on, speak on, and act on as a positive leader. Let this guide you through your daily life. Remember, this word will be the one that takes up the three to four spots in your mind. Let it resonate, let it inspire, and let it encourage you to become an ever-growing better positive leader.

For this to work, you will need to stay committed to it. Without the commitment to acting on what you think and speak, it becomes empty thoughts, empty words and unfulfilled potential. Your foundation of acting as a Positive THINK, SPEAK, ACT Leader is committing your actions to your thoughts and words.

Initiate: Act *Wrapped Up*

Action Science	Leadership burns calories.
Act Currency	Busy can kill productivity.
Connect What Is Disconnected	Follow through with your actions based on your thoughts and words.
Act It: Practical Exercise	The thoughts you have and the words you speak should align with your actions.
Leadership ACT	Be the example for others to follow.

ACTION & STEPS: Process Planning Notes

Question	Your Thoughts
Identify why you would "Act" differently?	
Investigate how you would elevate your "Act"?	
Initiate what would be your "Act"?	

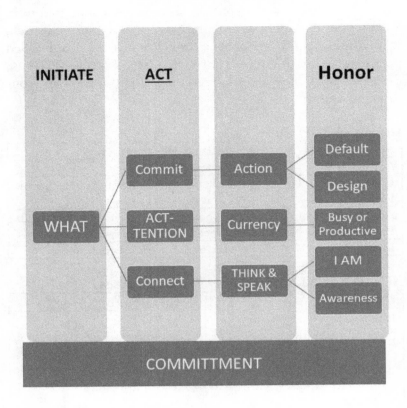

Chapter 6

GO SERVE EXPERIENCES

"I urge you to live a life worthy of the calling you have received." Ephesians 4:1

Nothing changes unless you do. If you do what you always did, you will get what you always got. How do you make these changes? It is your SHIFT! I firmly believe you should make changes, and not just any changes but positive changes through creating experiences. In my experiences, the most impactful way to make changes is through serving experiences. When you embrace the SHIFT of how you create experiences with others, you will find that you can do amazing things to and for others. As a leader, you have the opportunity to become a leader of serving experiences through servant leadership.

Stepping into the role of servant leadership can be a daunting revelation at first. In the traditional sense, most aspire to become a leader in order to climb to the top of the pyramid, bark orders and sit back while your organization or team does the heavy lifting. In that approach, how connected do you feel the organization or team will be to you as a leader with that style of traditional leadership approach? This model does little to inspire growth, positive change or increased productivity except through fear. When making a change to servant leadership, there is an endless potential of positive experiences waiting to be explored. Serving experiences as a servant leader is where you will find fulfillment in all that you think, speak and act. It becomes the fulfillment of your opportunities and for those around you.

I firmly believe the most important leader is one who does for the organization and team that may never be able to return the favor except through their own growth. How is this heart of a servant leader shaped and guided? The answer is

115

simple, a foundation based on a set of core values. The next question I hope you are thinking is not what is a core value because I am sure most know what it is (and if you don't I'll share a little bit about it in a minute), but do core values make a difference? The answer to this question is a resounding YES! If core values make a difference, then how does it connect to serving experiences? Core values become the how you serve the experiences. It is truly all connected.

Core Values

A lot of us recognize core values as a concept. Many organizations will have a set of core values along with their mission statement and possibly some other forms of statements on their company website or on a nice framed picture hanging on the wall in the office somewhere. It is those organizations that lean on and use the core values as their guiding principles that you find, more often than not, to be the more successful companies and organizations. Furthermore, those organizations that encourage their teams to know and internalize the core values, will find even greater success.

Core values become a guiding principle for the organization and team to think, speak and act if used properly. If faced with a problem or opportunity, the organization and team should immediately look to their core values and ensure that the decision, the words and actions they take will align with the core values. If it does not, then back to the drawing board.

Now truly is this real? Should a set of core values truly guide an organization and team to make decisions, speak certain ways and act in a certain manner? Absolutely! A person, team and organization that moves should be guided by a set of agreed-upon values that supports the organization and team in a positive and constructive manner. It should not be over-complicated or complex, simply words thoughtfully curated for the benefit of the organization, team and the ultimate experiences it wants to create for others. These values should give the organization and team pause to think, speak and act in a way that supports the values and creates certain experiences.

As a positive think, speak, act leader, the core values of the organization you support should align with your own. What do you mean to align with my own core values? Yes, you should have a set of your own core values that define how you create experiences for others. You do not have to be a company or organization to have a set of core values. A person or family can benefit from creating a core value system of their own. These core values will become what you stand for, not against, when you make decisions, speak words and act accordingly. The experiences you create for others through your core values will become how others know you.

There are a number of methods to create a set of core values you can find on the internet. Numerous different steps to take and thousands of "core value" words and statements to inspire you. This is a personal journey you experience as you identify, investigate and initiate your own set of core values. This is an intentional process that will take time and may develop as you go through them. Defining the core values you deem worthy of the experiences you will create, is personal. Living by them is intentional, takes responsibility on your part and will require accountability should you veer off your set of core values. Having a strong set of core values is at the heart of a servant leader.

Servant Leadership

Leading can be construed as moving things forward from a position of power. This is leading in its simplest form. As a leader, you can "make" someone do something or change from this perceived position of power, but the potential intrinsic change with your team is only temporary. Others are less likely to truly change until you serve as a leader. Serving is doing for others in the moment from a humble perspective. With an expectation for nothing in return except that the receiving person benefits, learns and grows as a result of the experience. This is servant leadership.

Let me clear up any misconception of servant leadership. When I mention serving others, doing for others in a humble perspective, I am not referring to a leader giving up their authority and becoming a hostage to their team by doing everything for them. On the contrary, a servant leader can maintain authority and still support their team to success. Servant leadership is about the support of their team or organization through the experiences, the struggles and successes. There is honor in serving as a servant leader.

A servant leader experience is probably one of the most transformational experiences you can do for another person or group of people. What does it mean to create a transformational experience? There is a big difference between transactional and transformational experiences. A Transactional experience is a one and done, nothing more, nothing less. Neither people involved are changed from this kind of experience. How do you become a servant leader to serve experiences and create transformational experiences?

Transformational Experiences

I'm going to let you in on a little secret. Understanding the differences between transactional and transformational leadership is one of the most impactful pieces in this book. This will be the hinge by which you will take your positive think, speak, act leadership to the next level. It is honor that is the lubricant that allows the hinge to work smoothly. It's important to recognize the differences between what we normally identify as leadership but is truly managing and the experiences created by both. Here we can compare the differences between two types of experiences.

Transactional (Manager)	Transformational (Leader)
One and done impression	Creates a lasting impression
Dictates	Inspires
Discourages	Encourages
Current State	Future State
Speaks to	Listens with
Sympathy	Empathy
Punishes	Supports
Closed-Minded	Open-Minded
Reluctant	Committed
Isolated	Community
Work-Style	Life-Style

A transactional leader or better labeled as a manager is there for the moment and for themselves. This manager is simply there to move and direct people to accomplish the task. There is no value added for the organization or team from a manager. They become great at checking boxes and completing tasks. Here is my to-do list for the day: check, check, check, done; time to go home. If a team member fails at a task, there is punishment and no support. If a team member wants to grow in their career, that becomes their own responsibility. There is no input from the team to make changes or improvements. The transactional leader ultimately creates a culture of working for the paycheck. Ultimately, there is no SHIFT.

Here is the hinge in which your Positive Think, Speak, Act Leadership door should swing on. Becoming a transformational leader creates value in three aspects: Intentionality, Responsibility and Accountability. Combining these three mindsets creates a path in which a leader will create a culture of commitment, higher morale, and ultimately increased performance from the organization and team. All three will go through the internal, external and overall leadership path to be internalized as a part of the organization and team culture. This is a major SHIFT in your approach. It all starts with a positive think, speak, act leader. You are not able to expect your organization or team to be intentional, responsible or accountable unless you display it first. Lead by example.

INTENTIONALITY

This is where a positive leader begins to become a transformational leader. It only occurs through your intentionality. How do you create a lasting impression with your team, inspire, encourage and all the other components of a transformation leader? It simply stems from using what you have filled your think, to speak it and then act on it. We all have these fleeting thoughts that cross through our minds that "I should" or "I could." Most of us rarely speak or act on it because of one reason or another. This is the point in which intentionality should take over and you speak and act on the "I should" and "I could." It is odd at first and will build easier as you let it be intentional in a design manner. Let's start with an easy approach.

Never use the word "just" in front of your leadership. Your leadership is more than "just" anything. Don't let "just" anything identify your leadership, this is a negative approach word. Your value is way beyond that. Your impact is too great and too valuable to diminish it with "just". Using "just" as your adjective describes you as average. If you have made it this far in the book, you are not average. Let me repeat that, you are NOT average. As Keith Craft shares, "don't let good rob you of better." You have to be intentional to be more than average or set on default.

Without 'just' in our descriptors and vocabulary that leaves us the option to do things terribly or with excellence. So, let me ask you, would you rather be known for doing things terribly or with excellence? What you think, what you speak, what you do is your calling card, it is your reputation. You build yourself intentionally along the way by the way you think, speak and act. Be intentionally excellent. Your organization and team will see it.

Another example of becoming a transformational leader is through the experiences you create with your organization and team.   It's ok to be the cheerleader, it's ok to inspire and encourage others. Take a moment to listen when your team is speaking with you and empathize when they are struggling. Be supportive and open-minded when they share a new idea or concept. Be committed to the organization and team. These acts stem from having a positive think that allows you to speak and act with a transformational approach. When you walk into a room, others should know it, feel it, welcome it and leave better because of you being there. You intentionally set the atmosphere and mood and not react to it. It simply takes making it happen, listening to the voice in your mind that says, "I should" or "I could" and do it intentionally.

RESPONSIBILITY

It's not just about you. It's about the people around you. The organization around you.   There is a responsibility for yourself and what is around you to lead for a greater purpose. Even if you're leading a team of cashiers or a board of directors, lead to understand that you are responsible for the way you think, speak and act and that the organization and team are responsible for the way they think, speak and act. When you recognize this, leading becomes different and impactful. Responsibility is the ongoing duty a transformational leader has to be the positive think, speak, act leader for their organization and team.

Tim Elmore is quoted as saying, "I can assure you, most emphatically, that you have more impact than you realize. 'Sociologists tell us the most introverted of people will influence 10,000 others in an average lifetime.' Imagine how many people you have knowingly and unknowingly influenced in your life so far." That is a lot of responsibility when you think about it. The things you think, speak and act could potentially impact, influence, direct at least 10,000 people in a lifetime. As we mentioned earlier, you are beyond average. Whether you are introverted or an extrovert or an ambivert, your above average impact can go well beyond 10,000 people.

As mentioned earlier you have a duty to be the positive think, speak, act leader for your organization and team. The word duty is an interesting word. You hear this in the context of the military, and rarely outside that realm. I encourage you to take up your responsibility of having a duty to your organization and team. A responsibility to become better and take your organization and team with you on the journey. This is a commitment or expectation of your core values. Be honorable to others because you are honorable and allow your defined core values to steer your intentionality.

ACCOUNTABILITY

Sometimes as a leader, you take the hit. You take one for the team. The leader is accountable not only for themselves, but they are also accountable for the team and organization. You are accountable for the results and outcome. Accountability is what happens after a situation has occurred. This is the effect of the situation. Leaders need to have thick skin and a big heart.

Within an organization, taking accountability is not personal, its leadership. You are not defined by the failures, only how you respond to them and recover. There is no blaming or complaining here.

When your organization and team recognize that you, as the positive think, speak, act leader, are accountable for the process and outcome, there is confidence in you as the leader. It is not that the team feels comfortable because they can hide behind the leader when things go bad, they have confidence that if things go bad, their leader is there to take it and lead the team together to learn, grow through it and be better the next time an issue comes around the corner. It's not them in failure, it's me as the accountable leader and it is not me as the winner, it's us as the accountable leaders. You take the hit in the bad and share the praise in the good. These are the experiences your team will value and stand with you.

Serving experiences as a leader is powerful. There is a myriad of benefits when a leader is transformational versus transactional. Experiences are what people remember from the interaction with the leader, organization and team. I have always been fascinated by how and what we remember from our experiences.

Experience Place Holders

Imagine that our memories from past experiences are placed in place holders in our minds. Most would either fall into a good, meh or bad compartment or place holder. Now imagine each place holder as a box holding the individual memories of each individual past experiences and emotions.

As emotion stems from experiences, we categorize these emotions within our memories. Shahram Heshmat Ph D. in his article, "Why Do We Remember Certain Things, But Forget Others?" describes how the "normal function of emotion is to enhance memory in order to improve recall of experiences that have important or relevance for our survival." In other words, experiences that create emotion (positive or negative) are the ones that we will have a tendency to remember because of the impact or value of that experience.

With a human tendency to have a negative bias, the place holder that holds the "bad" experiences will be filled much more than the other two boxes. These memories will be heavy and collect at the bottom of the place holder, some will merge with other "bad" experiences creating an even heavier one like a black hole of "bad". If we allow it, the "bad" experiences can continue to collect and eventually take over everything. Even though the experiences in this place holder are heavy they are easy to access. There is no password or combination to get into the "bad" place holder. In fact, this place holder is open all the time, waiting for one "bad" experience to be accessed by a simple doubting thought or questioning circumstance. A popular saying is "you are only as good as your last mistake" (read as "bad"). Holding on to this quote keeps your "bad" experiences at the forefront. The place holder has a lot of holes in it allowing for these "bad" experiences to leak out of the "bad" place holder and into another place holder. These "bad" leaks can corrupt a "meh" or even a "good" experience.

The "meh" experiences are "just there" experience. Neither exciting, scary, happy or sad. Just there... And this place holder is almost invisible. It's hard to find it in your memories. These are the experiences in which we go through on autopilot, passively allowing things to happen to us without much input. This is your default mindset approach. There are not a lot of experiences in this box because they are less important and not worth remembering. They do not collect or do anything to any of the other two experiences. When the failure experiences leak into this box, there is not much activity or corruption. The "bad" experiences do not bother the "meh" too much because there is little value in the "meh". A "bad" experience would not create much of an impact if it corrupted it because intrinsically there is little there already. The "good" experience is not concerned with the "meh". It will avoid it because it is more concerned with the design approach and feels sad that the "meh" experiences were potentially wasted opportunities.

Depending on your approach to life, either by default or design, the "good" experience place holder can vary in volume.

Depending on your view of being considered humble or egotistical, this place holder can be tough to access or way too easy to access. The "good" experiences are light and tend to gather to the top with the most recent success always sitting at the top of the place holder. Our "good" are the experiences that we lean on to support our right to feel good about ourselves in a lot of circumstances. We use these on our resumes to help get a job, we use these to impress a certain person that we want to like us. Or reflect on these when you are feeling bad. Our "good" experiences are what we like to share with others (read social media).

Now imagine as you look at the experience place holders, you apply a filter over all of it. Based on your filter or perception of the experiences you can either create false or distorted views or move experiences around into different place holders. All experiences can change over time or through suggestion. In some instances, the good, meh and bad can move to different place holders. This happens when we adjust our perception or filter and revisit the experiences.

It is possible to maneuver each life experience into the "good" place holder if you apply a "Positive THINK, SPEAK, ACT" filter. If you apply this filter to each experience and learn from it and grow through what you go through, then each experience becomes a potential success or "good" experience.

Now understanding your own place holders of experiences and memories, what experiences are you creating for others? Do your thoughts, speech and actions simply create a "meh" experience that will be lost in a short time? Are you creating "bad" experiences that others will hold onto and let surface when they think about you? Or do you intentionally, based on your positive THINK, SPEAK, ACT approach, create experiences for others that will fill and overflow their "good" place holder. Do you find ways even in the most mundane interactions with others to provide better and positive experiences than is expected? Each experience you have with another person is your calling card. When you internalize The SUPERFANTASTIC Process, this is your calling as a Positive

THINK, SPEAK, ACT Leader to become and do more for others.

All of these thoughts, spoken words, actions and experiences are a process. Many will continue to look for success to create a result. But I believe a lot of people chase the tail or let the tail wag the dog in this search for better things. When we recognize that if we are faithful in an approach to be positive, supportive of ourselves and others, then and only then are we successful. Success does not cause happiness rather happiness causes success. Or rather success does not cause positivity, positivity causes success. A positive transformational experience given to another person as a servant leader stems from happiness and will create more success than imaginable. When you give, you will receive more than a double share. When you are a leader you are called to live a life worthy of the title you have earned and entrusted to you. Serving experiences guided by your core values with intentionality, responsibility and accountability will do more for you and those around you than you can ever imagine. Go serve others and there you will find your reward.

When you arrive to serving experiences, you will find that you will become part of the experiences as well. Some of the experiences you serve for others will impact you as much as it impacts others. These transformational moments will connect the entire process for you as a Positive THINK, SPEAK, ACT Leader. In this moment you will begin to review all the previous steps within the process. Transformational experiences of serving others will encourage and inspire you to go back and identify your why, which will lead you to investigate your how and ultimately investigate your what so that you can elevate your future transformational experiences serving others. This SUPERFANTASTIC process is truly a cycle of layering and building on your experiences stemming from each step. Develop the SUPER in you so that you can create the FANTASTIC around you. Do not let it end here, grow with it as you go through it. You are meant for more, you are meant to fulfill the calling you have on your life as a Positive THINK, SPEAK, ACT Leader.

Go Serve Experiences *Wrapped Up*

Servant Leadership	Serving is doing for others with no expectation of repayment except for them to improve.
Transformational Experiences	The hinge of The SUPERFANTASTIC Process.
Intentionality	Do the "I could" and "I should".
Responsibility	Recognize your ongoing duty.
Accountability	Taking the hit.
Experience Place Holders	Experience matters for it to be remembered.

ACTION & STEPS: Process Planning Notes

Question	Your Thoughts
Identify why you would "Go Serve Experiences?"	
Investigate how you would "Go Serve Experiences?"	
Initiate what would be your "Go Serve Experiences?"	

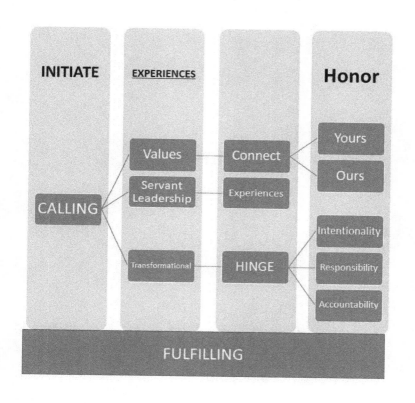

"For nothing is impossible with God."

Luke 1:37

Chapter 7

WRAPPED UP

Even though this is the final chapter in the book, it is truly the first chapter for you.

You now have the opportunity to write your own story, your own experiences and ultimately your own success. From here you have the tools and resources to become a Positive THINK, SPEAK, ACT Leader. I have intentionally presented this book as a process to follow, a SUPERFANTASTIC process if you will. It is an inside out approach. This subtitle is intentional in its order as well. It presents a process in which to follow. The order of the chapters is presented in a process intentionally to allow you to identify, investigate and eventually initiate what you internalize.

Show me why, how and what a person THINKS, SPEAKS and ACTS, and I'll show you the potential for their success. In this book, I have shared a wealth of information with you. My goal with this book is to provide a manual for new and existing leaders (and remember we are all leaders) to become a positive THINK, SPEAK, ACT leader. It has been presented in a process so that you can follow it step by step. If you remember from earlier, I am a process person, and this is a template for you to follow for your own journey. Here you can identify, investigate and initiate this, The SUPERFANTASTIC Process.

We spent time identifying Positivity and Leadership. Jumped into investigating Positive Leadership. Then pushed towards initiating Think, Speak and Act. As a bonus, we added Go Serve Experiences.

Let's wrap up this process of becoming a positive Think, Speak, Act leader. Each chapter is a process that should be intentional. For it to be successful take responsibility for thinking on it, speaking on it and acting on it and creating the experiences from it. Know each step in the process that will take you to your next level.

- Positive
- Leadership
- Positive Leadership
- Think
- Speak
- Act
- Go Serve Experiences

How do you sustain the fix? This is one of the questions asked of me by one of my leaders that changed my perspective on change. I never thought about it before, that deeply, until I was asked that question. What is the purpose of changing or improving something unless you can sustain it? A design approach is not easy. A default approach is comfortable and the easy way out. When you commit to sustaining the fix, you commit to a design approach. This requires of you a new way of perceiving your world. Use the tools shared within The SUPERFANTASTIC Principles to sustain the fix. Alignments and mentors are your check value in sustaining the fix. The rest is up to you. Remember, how you think about yourself, is how you will think about others. How you speak about yourself, is how you will speak about others. How you act towards yourself, is how you will act to others. How you honor yourself is eventually how you will honor others.

What is your ROI on all of this? Time of crisis and stress do not create problems as much as they reveal them. Crisis and stress will expose the true nature of a leader's positive think, speak and act. Your ROI from developing, building and creating yourself as a positive think, speak, act leader will stem from you leading the example for yourself and others in good times and bad. In the bad times is when an organization and team need their leader to be the positive think, speak, act leader. Your ROI through this is creating overall leadership within your organization through your process of internal leadership and external leadership. The ideal situation to create is overall leadership. Your team is now duplicating what you have been working towards for so long. It is a process, and this will not be easy. And you are more than just another leader. You are THE SUPERFANTASTIC Process: Positive Think, Speak, Act Leader!

As a final experiment I want to leave you with, let's continue to internalize it all. Before we end this process let's fill in the blanks, let's think, speak and act on part four of our in-book experiment. This is all you. Your mind is discovering your THINK. Your words are developing your SPEAK. Your actions are deploying your ACT. Commit to it here and now. If you don't do it now, when will you? This is your moment to decide if The SUPERFANTASTIC Process is for you. This is your moment of SHIFT. Are you willing to THINK, SPEAK and ACT your way to success? What do you have to lose? Or better said, imagine your possible ROI on becoming the Positive Think, Speak, Act Leader. This is for you.

THINK:
I am [insert positive leadership word]!
SPEAK:
I am [insert positive leadership word]!
ACT:
I am [insert positive leadership word]!

This is the end of this book. I pray you will continue to live a life worthy of your calling and fill your mind with good things so that you can speak and act in good deeds for you and those around you. I pray you become The SUPERFANTASTIC leader that this world needs and have been placed in this world to be for others. You are a special person, a special leader with unique and precious gifts given to you to do things that no one else in this world can do. I pray The SUPERFANTASTIC Process transforms you to become the positive THINK, SPEAK, ACT Leader fulfilling your potential.

The SUPERFANTASTIC Process

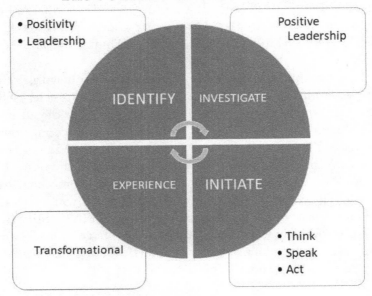

YOU'RE NOT DONE YET... NOW WHAT?

I want to express a SUPERFANTASTIC thank you for reading this book. Most importantly the trust you gave me to spend your most precious resource and time on this book. It does not go unrecognized. So now what?

There are two types of people that read books. Most people would be satisfied with simply reading this book, hoping they will retain enough and make a minimal effort to embrace The SUPERFANTASTIC Process and become a Positive THINK, SPEAK, ACT Leader. However, I imagine you are not like most people. You are above average and looking to elevate your THINK, SPEAK and ACT. If I can provide you with support to continue to grow as a Positive THINK, SPEAK, ACT Leader, would you consider at least giving it a look? Do me a favor and check out my website at www.TheGaryGregory.com for more support to become a Positive THINK, SPEAK, ACT Leader. Do yourself a favor and check it out.

Just one more thing, did I mention there is a link to a FREE checklist you can use to become the Positive THINK, SPEAK, ACT Leader you were called to become.

Answer to the Question from the Introduction:

As promised, the leader that ended up changing the world with incredible leadership examples lived thousands of years ago. This leader came for you and for me. Everything said, every move, every story, every example closely scrutinized, followed and loved, for us. He had twelve close followers (and one that betrayed him) and a group of followers that grew exponentially all over the world. This leader was Jesus Christ, my Lord and Savior. Jesus was a leader that had a process that was beyond SUPERFANTASTIC. A process that was divinely inspired. He knew the end result for his earthly life, but the ongoing result was promised to be so much more.

Chapter 7   WRAPPED UP

Chapter 7   WRAPPED UP

Chapter 7   WRAPPED UP

ACKNOWLEDGEMENTS

Leaders, by nature, are flawed. Writers, by nature, are flawed as well. People, in general, are flawed. It is what makes us human and so special at the same time. But these flaws have a purpose for a greater good. If, in our course of Think, Speak, Act, we identify and investigate our flaws, then we have an even greater responsibility to initiate growth. And not just any growth, positive growth. This does not happen alone. Sometimes our personal and professional flaws are difficult to see, even if it is staring right back at us in the mirror. It takes a team. A team of right alignments make the journey even better than the finish line. I would like to recognize my team, my alignments that continuously help me recognize my flaws, recognize my opportunities and inspire me to be better today than I was yesterday;

Jesus Christ, my Lord and Savior. I would be lost without; I was blind, but now I see. All glory to God.

MaryAnn, my bride, for putting up with me and supporting me for so many years. For looking at me funny when I share my dreams and thoughts, challenging me to be better and still supporting me along the way. For stepping in, filling in the gaps and championing for our family to be a family.

Griffin, Wyatt, Sophia and Virginia are my four amazing kids with whom I a blessed to be their dad. They never cease to amaze and inspire me.

Mom and Dad for being the loving and supportive parents. My first examples of leadership. No matter what I do: good, bad or ugly, you have always supported me with a kind word or stern redirection when needed.

Pastor Keith Craft (keithcraft.org) is my spiritual father and Elevate Life Church (www.elevate.life) is my home. This is what loving people into life-long transformation looks like. I am beyond blessed to be part of this family of choice.

Mighty Men are my brothers in this world. There for support, correction and redirection when needed. Iron sharpening iron.

Mike Rodriguez (www.mikerodriguezinternational.com) is the man, the myth and legend to me. He is responsible for encouraging me and helping me see things in a new and bigger perspective. That NOW will forever be the best time to make things happen.

Leaders in my career journey both past and present. These are the people that have forged the path ahead of me, corrected and redirected me, taught me, inspired me, encouraged me and given me all the second (and sometimes more) chances to be better. Thank you to Terry, Laura, Hara, Dawn, Deanna, Rhonda, Ric, Keith, Susan, Allison, Mark, Kip, Tiffany, Randy, Rod, and so many others.

Fred Blumenberg (www.TheRealFredLee.com) is one of the most positive people I know. Blessed that I found him and made a connection. His authentic positivity is what makes a positive difference in this world.

It is an honor to have these alignments and more in my life. Thank you all for all that you do, for the glory that God has put in you to be in this world to make a positive impact on others. You are a gift to this world (and me) and for that, I humbly and gratefully thank you.

The SUPERFANTASTIC Process

The SUPERFANTASTIC Process

ABOUT THE AUTHOR
"Today is the day the Lord has made; we will rejoice and be glad in it."
Psalms 118:24

I grew up in Houston in a quiet suburban neighborhood and blessed with two solid and supportive parents. I was a nerdy kid throughout school, afraid to go beyond my boundaries and make mistakes. Eventually, I ventured to the University of Houston where there was a new world to explore beyond the suburbs. I decided to look for opportunities to change and grow when I got to college (though I never quite lost the nerdy description if you ask many of my friends).

While in college, I spent a lot of time trying to find the right fit in a new and bigger world. Distracted by all the new experiences and opportunities, school and studying were not on the list of priorities. I eventually found my stride after focusing on a business major. I was incredibly blessed to find my future wife (and eventually a college degree).

After graduating from college and then getting married, I explored several different kinds of work. While in Houston I worked retail for a while and then started traveling the country teaching computer software for car dealerships. With my wife and firstborn, we moved to El Paso where I taught GED English and worked in a BINGO hall. Texas A&M University-Corpus Christi called for an opportunity to manage student housing and on occasion, I valet parked cars. We moved from the desert to the beach. Finally, we moved to Dallas for a go at managing multi-family apartments. While in Dallas I joined an amateur triathlon racing team and started a personal training business during this time as well. Each move around the state and career opportunity was an attempt to fill a void or purpose I could not fill.

It was not until I stepped foot in a church in 2015 that I began to find out what was most important in my life, my purpose. My eyes were opened, and I realized what I was missing, the void I was trying to fill was to be filled there. With

Pastor Keith Craft and the alignments made through Elevate Life Church, I have devoted my life to better things and changing my filter and perception. Each day is a chance to fight the good fight alongside God, my wife, my children and my family of choice. My boundaries and opportunities are now limitless. My purpose is found.

You will find my approach in life and leadership will have a biblical perspective and approach. I am by no means perfect and continuously work on developing my relationship with God to help me become better.

The SUPERFANTASTIC Process is a follow up to The SUPERFANTASTIC Principles. Both books can stand alone in their lessons, and together they do so much more. The order is intentional and the foundation of the SUPERFANTASTIC is biblical with practical application. My experiences, encounters and testimony help tell the story along the way.

Speak Life to Your Success at www.TheGaryGregory.com. Available for coaching, speaking, training and encouragement.

All glory to God for the processes He gives us in His word.

Disclaimer & Copyright Information

The content shared should not be considered guaranteed or fool-proof for business or life change.

REFERENCES

Finding Your Why: Discover Your Purpose, Mike Rodriguez

The 5 Second Rule, Mel Robbins

The SUPERFANTASTIC Principles, Gary Gregory

https://engineering.mit.edu/engage/ask-an-engineer/what-are-thoughts-made-of/

https://www.sciencedaily.com/terms/thought.htm

https://positivepsychology.com/positive-leadership/

https://www.mcgill.ca/engage/files/engage/authentic_leadership_avolio_gardner_2005.pdf

https://www.mayoclinic.org/healthy-lifestyle/stress-management/in-depth/positive-thinking/art-20043950

https://www.nm.org/healthbeat/healthy-tips/11-fun-facts-about-your-brain

https://www.forbes.com/sites/forbescoachescouncil/2017/10/16/what-is-your-impact/#714352b26f35

https://www.forbes.com/sites/kathycaprino/2014/06/02/9-core-behaviors-of-people-who-positively-impact-the-world/#7304969e6b41

https://www.hcli.org/articles/five-ways-lead-responsibly-hclis-new-ceo

https://thejoyjunkie.com/5-ways-to-check-yourself-before-you-wreck-yourself/

https://www.psychologytoday.com/us/blog/heartache-hope/201407/the-importance-checking-in-yourself

https://www.popsugar.com/fitness/how-to-check-in-with-yourself-when-youre-feeling-stressed-46723707

https://www.drireneonline.com/self-development-taking-personal-inventory

https://www.16personalities.com/

https://www.psychologytoday.com/us/blog/science-choice/201510/why-do-we-remember-certain-things-forget-others

CPSIA information can be obtained
at www.ICGtesting.com
Printed in the USA
LVHW010152100221
678885LV00003B/496